Harriet Love's Guide to
VINTAGE CHIC

HARRIET LOVE

Harriet Love's Guide to VINTAGE CHIC

With photographs by Gustavo Candelas

HOLT, RINEHART AND WINSTON · NEW YORK

Copyright © 1982 by Harriet Love
Photographs by Gustavo Candelas Copyright © 1980, 1981.
All rights reserved, including the right to reproduce this book
or portions thereof in any form.
Published by Holt, Rinehart and Winston,
383 Madison Avenue, New York, New York 10017
Published simultaneously in Canada by Holt, Rinehart and
Winston of Canada, Limited.

Library of Congress Cataloging in Publication Data

Love, Harriet.
   Harriet Love's Guide to vintage chic.
   1. Clothing and dress.   I. Title.   II. Title: Guide
to vintage chic.   III. Title: Vintage chic.
TT560.L68   646'.34   82-1040
                        AACR2

ISBN Hardbound: 0-03-056238-4
ISBN Paperback: 0-03-056239-2

First Edition

Designer: Jacqueline Schuman
Printed in the United States of America

10 9 8 7 6 5 4 3 2 1

ISBN 0-03-056238-4 HARDBOUND
ISBN 0-03-056239-2 PAPERBACK

to Asher D. Jason

Contents

Acknowledgments

A great debt goes to Dorothy Schefer for her outstanding special consultation on this project; and to Gustavo Candelas for his beautiful photographs, which represent two and a half years of work. Many thanks to my agents, Deborah Geltman and Gayle Benderoff, for their many hours of consultation and support; to Mary Peacock for her ideas and editorial work; and to Natalie Chapman, a super editor, for her vision, devotion, and enthusiasm.

This book could not have been completed without the voluntary hard work of many friends and business associates. My heartfelt thanks to Patricia Anichini, Shirley Bach, The Bettmann Archive, Carol Bovoso, Jean Butler, Jill Candelas, Ilene Chazanof, Robert Christian, Christie's East, David Cohen, Julie Collier, Dorissa Curry, Gina Davis, Christian Dior, Susan Dollenmaier, Mike Dykeman, Elite Modeling Agency, Sarah Fields, Billy Frank, Marilis Flusser, Durell Godfrey, Jean Gold, Barbara Greenwald, Eliot Hubbard, Cassandra Hughes, Raymond Jurado, Robert Kitchens, Hedy Klineman, Truusje Kushner, Carol Lavin, Pam Leon, Jerry Lieberman, Ron Lieberman, Susan Lieberman, Elaine Louie, Ben Love, Rose Love, Madonna, Nina Malkin, Keiko Miyasaka, Julie Myers, Ed Netherton, Colombe Nicholas, Suzanne Noble, Peggy O'Dea, Alexandra Penney, Phyllis Posnick, Rochelle Redfield, Linda Rodin, Larry Russell, Fred Seidman, Kathleen Seltzer, Debbi Shapiro, Janet Siefert, Dyanne Silver, Robert W. Skinner Gallery Inc., Patti Smith, Suzanne Srlamba, Alice Stauber, Norman Stevens, Amanda Stinchecum, Carol Troy, and Joan Vass.

Harriet Love's Guide to VINTAGE CHIC

Introduction

When I began in this business in 1965, the only thing that could be said about vintage clothing was that it was old and used and that you had to be a little weird or theatrical to buy it, let alone wear it on days other than Halloween. Today every fashion-conscious woman and man has probably bought at least one old piece and worn it as evening or everyday clothing. In recent years vintage apparel has become a unique style of dress for people without a huge fashion allowance. And many with thousands of dollars to spend still find that the only time anyone else looks at them at a party is when they have on a special find from their favorite vintage-clothing shop.

My first customers seventeen years ago were young actresses and artists with very little money, theatrical taste, and very low clothing budgets. Some of them worked part-time and went to fashion schools at night. Many well-known painters expressed their interest in textiles by wearing old paisley shawls or silkscreened dresses to art openings. The average person's reaction to this "fashion statement" was curiosity and often criticism. But people who want to be original have always paid little attention to the criticism and appreciated the curiosity.

As more antique-clothing stores opened during the seventies and were written up in fashion magazines, the public became more aware of vintage clothing. They tested the water by buying a scarf or an accessory. The cost at this time was still minimal. If a shawl didn't work out, if a blouse tore under the arm, or if the color was wrong for your skin tone, you just shoved it into the back of your closet along with other, more expensive new-clothes rejects. The cost of such a mistake was only about five dollars and nothing to get too upset about. Now that the five-dollar clothing purchase has gone the way of the 35-cent slice of pizza, our decisions have to be more carefully thought out.

When vintage clothes first began being sold by a few shops in the late sixties, you could have the pick of the Victorian blouse rack, for example, in perfect condition and for very little money. A perfect-condition Chinese or Spanish shawl with multicolored embroidery was $30. That great wedding dress your friend made from hand-embroidered batiste and real lace was $25.

Finding old clothes is not the cheap thrill it used to be in the sixties. No more thrift-shop bargains and naive flea-market dealers . . . no more auctions where you can find "everything in this box, for the lucky lady who sews at home, ten dollars." The message is out: Old clothes are not the same as secondhand clothes. They are fashion. They are collectible. Like antiques, they're being sold in shops across the United States and in Europe; they're even being auctioned at Christie's East and Sotheby's.

Today, when the price of a decent new wardrobe practically requires a second mortgage on your house, antique clothing still costs less than comparable new clothes. And vintage clothes are much more accessible today in shops, auctions, flea markets, even some department stores, than they were ten years ago.

Still, customers treasure the name of a favorite antique-clothing shop, keeping its location a closer secret than the name of their plastic surgeon. After years of hearing new customers ask, "When did you open?" and hearing myself answer, "Seventeen years ago," I am used to their surprise that my business is so old.

Surprisingly enough, many people who would enjoy shopping for and wearing antique clothing resist it, finding the shops difficult to browse and buy in. Displayed items are often one of a kind; the boutique owner looks costumed; there are too many things to choose from; the sizes are confusing; styles are unique and too varied; things are not always in good condition.

1

No one can blame the consumer for being confused. Shopping for vintage clothing *is* different and requires adjustment. Which is why I have written this book. It is a guide to antique clothing: what to buy, where to find it, how to care for it, how to put it together. With lots of tips, hints, secrets revealed. Shopping for and wearing antique clothes has always been one of my favorite pastimes—as well as my business. It has become for me what crossword puzzles are for other addicts. My husband has always said of me that nothing would make me happier after I died than to go to a never-ending old-clothes flea market in the sky.

Next to buying and wearing old clothes, nothing makes me happier than talking about this business and helping other people relish its delights. So enjoy. And good hunting!

P A R T   O N E

Getting Acquainted

What Is Vintage Clothing?

It has only been during the past few years that retailers other than thrift shops and a handful of devoted specialty stores have sold vintage clothing. Museums show antique clothes in textile and costume exhibits, and collectors buy their early-nineteenth-century finds and tuck them away. But for the consumer the concept is a new one: Old clothes that look new and fresh are shown in a boutique setting and are worn in a contemporary way.

Usually the word *antique* means anything that is over one hundred years old. But since this book is primarily about twentieth-century clothing, it seems appropriate to use a word that better describes what we're talking about: *vintage*.

And while we're clarifying terms, the first big hang-up we have to deal with is the word *secondhand*. Many potential converts to old clothes cannot bear the idea of wearing something someone has already owned and worn. Some people are hung up on whether the clothes are really "clean" and free of dirt and germs. Even people who seem to have no objection to lending their clothes to friends and friends of friends seem to have trouble with wearing clothes that once belonged to strangers.

Fortunately the stigma attached to buying "secondhand" began to disappear when young college students, with very little money for imaginative wardrobes, caught on to thrift-shop possibilities in the late fifties and early sixties. And hesitation over cleanliness might well disappear altogether if everyone were to realize that dry cleaning includes a sterilization process, which should dispel the myth that you can catch another's diseases.

The other stigma attached to secondhand clothing has nothing to do with cleanliness. It's a myth that I like to call "bad-vibes jive." Who was the person who owned this dress? What was she like? How do I know what she did in these clothes? Did she die a horrible death? And what do I need someone else's weird vibes around me for? This, of course, is ridiculous, yet I'm constantly surprised by how many people have voiced these superstitions to me when buying secondhand.

I have always felt the opposite. That's probably why I enjoy this business so much. For me there is a sense of excitement and discovery in wearing someone else's blazer. I've found countless delights nestled in old pockets and purses—coins, theater tickets, photographs. More than once I've opened an old purse to find a dance card with few names on it—and I'm touched by this poor wallflower's life. The history one could write from some of the clothes I've worn or sold to others would probably be a lot more lively than the one we read about in high-school texts.

Being able to pick and choose from all the different styles of the past is what really got me hooked on vintage clothing. For someone who isn't familiar with the old-clothes market, this is hard to imagine. You can choose a white linen nightgown from the Edwardian era or a satin version from the thirties, cut on the bias to give a slinky effect. A hacking jacket originally worn for horseback riding can work for you with a new pair of pants or a straight skirt. A gray flannel blazer from the forties may be just the right thing to pair with the fifties plaid skirt you never threw away. Beaded blouses, sequined boleros, crepe de chine scarves, satin and lace bed jackets, alligator and needlepoint purses, Edwardian camisoles and petticoats . . . you can mix all the decades in a surprising and imaginative way so that your wardrobe is never dull and predictable.

Perhaps the best part of old clothing is that it was usually made with care and love, using special details and hand-finishing techniques that are prohibitively expensive today, with fabric and labor costs increasing every other month. You can find real lace and embroidery, handmade buttons, unusual dye techniques and hand coloration, roomier cuts, hand knitting, and one-of-a-kind custom pieces, all of which will be discussed in the chapters to come.

Another attraction of vintage clothing is the quality of fabric. The old, tightly woven cotton, silk, and wool is prized by many buyers. And so is

rayon, which is not only a much older fabric than most people realize but also not a synthetic; the fiber comes from cellulose. Most of the original hand-screened Hawaiian shirts are rayon, as are many of the best print dresses shown on these pages.

The challenge is finding the best merchandise, in good condition, and the fun is making it work with your individual style and personal approach to fashion.

One last myth about old-clothing aficionados: They are not hippies, matrons, or actors. They are contemporary working people interested in fashion. Few would choose to live with a complete antique wardrobe. Therefore, many photographs in the book show old and new clothing worn together, to give you plenty of ideas about how to mix what you have in your wardrobe with a few antique things. How to mix and match eras and styles and how to create classic looks for yourself and your own imagination are what this book is about.

Much of the intimidation shoppers feel around antique clothing is mistrust of sound, intuitive response. Craftsmanship, beauty, and stylized design should bring oohs and ahhs to our lips, but we don't trust these natural responses because so much fashion and style of the moment has been dictated to us. Some current fashions are ugly. Others work only for thin, tall women, leaving shorter or fatter women with nothing attractive to wear. We mustn't lose our ability to stick with classics if we prefer them, to wear red if we like it, to wear white in winter or velvet in spring, if it suits our individual tastes.

Reclaim your natural—and intuitive—good sense. Build on that with imagination, with ideas from books and articles and people you see on the street. But keep in mind that what you like comes first. It is an exciting and creative step to depend on your own visual judgment. Learning how to shop in antique-clothing boutiques and flea markets requires that you develop and trust your natural and intuitive good sense.

2

One Hundred Years of Fashion: A Short History

This book is not a history of fashion, nor is it an essay on fashion philosophy. It's a book about the antique-clothing business, which has become something of a phenomenon in the last ten to fifteen years. It's about how old fashions become new fashions . . . and about style and ingenuity. To have a better perspective on where fashion is going, it's helpful to know where it has been.

The Victorian Period (1837–1901)

Both the English and the French made fashion history during the Victorian era, but to simplify matters most people refer to clothing up to 1900 as Victorian. Interestingly, even the French royalty were dressed by an Englishman during the mid-Victorian period. The famous couture House of Worth was founded in Paris in 1858 by Charles Fredrick Worth, from Lincolnshire, England. Today his clothing is coveted by museums, designers, and private collectors.

When we think of Victorian clothing we think of handmade lace, delicate hand embroidery on silks, hand-finished hems, and hand-beaded outfits. But it was also during this period that two machines revolutionized clothing: a mechanical loom invented by Joseph Jacquard for weaving patterned fabrics, and the American invention of the sewing machine by Elias Howe.

Men's clothing during the Victorian period underwent a transition from colorful fabric, suppressed waists, and knee-length pants to the newer shapes of modern men's dress today. Black silk knee britches were still sometimes worn for evening till the turn of the century, and the dinner coat—called the tuxedo in the United States since it was first worn in Tuxedo Park, New York—first appeared in the 1880s. Trouser legs gradually widened, pants were creased by the 1890s, and cuffs came into vogue about 1900—the result of turning up trouser legs on rainy days to avoid mud. Shirt collars evolved from standing points to the turned-up collar, and elaborately tied cravats became neckties. Sportswear appeared, including the English staple—the tweed suit. And in the 1880s men began to sleep in pajamas (a Chinese import) instead of long nightshirts.

Victorian women had abandoned the loose-waisted Empire style of the early nineteenth century and returned to boned and fitted waists with full, flouncy skirts that, by 1860, measured ten yards around. A few years later the cagelike steel-hoop frames called crinolines began to fall from fashion; by 1870, they had evolved into the bustle.

The first sign of mannish style in women's clothes appeared in the 1880s in the form of a tailored suit, which took a firm hold on fashion and is still going strong. It was worn then with a small string tie and a plain shirt. And although women became more active in sports toward the end of the nineteenth century, they persisted in wearing heavily boned, tightly laced corsets to create an "hourglass" figure with an eighteen-inch waist—a look so familiar in the 1890s. Day dresses were simpler than ever, but their bell-shaped skirts ended in trains and were worn even for

Counterclockwise, starting opposite top: *Woman in full Victorian regalia: ruffled lace, hourglass fit, accessorized with parasol and brimmed hat. Gibson Girls of the turn of the century with typical leg-o'-mutton sleeves and the desirable tiny waists. Nice young ladies of 1905 wore soft, white cotton blouses and long skirts on spring afternoons. A pre-twenties loose look: no boned corset, no tiny waist.*

walking. Evening gowns were in the "princess style"—very fitted and gored from neck to hem. And the leg-o'-mutton sleeve (fuller at the top and tapering at the wrist) returned and grew to exaggerated proportion, replacing the fitted sleeve, fashionable since mid-century.

The well-accessorized woman was never caught without her parasol to shield her from the sun. It's surprising that parasols have not yet returned as a fashion item, considering the continual media reports on the dangers of too much sun.

From a fashion viewpoint, the nineteenth century ended with the death of Queen Victoria in 1901. Welcome Edward VII and the twentieth century.

The Look of 1900–1920: Out of the Trenches

I think we imagine that men's clothing must have changed as much as women's did in the early part of the twentieth century, but it didn't. Day and evening clothing was standardized, with strict codes about how to wear it, and the styles still came from London tailors. Although men's trousers took on fullness and then returned to a slimmer style, and shoulder shapes went from broad and padded to natural—a conservative style that has persisted through the decades—the only radical change that took place was in underwear. Men went from wearing long johns or union suits to sleeveless T-shirts and shorts.

The trench coat was introduced after World War I and became a household word; and the chesterfield coat was established as the dress coat. Men tried turtleneck and colorful Fair Isle sweaters in sportier moments.

While men's fashion changed in the shape and styling of the shoulders, women's fashion concentrated on changing the shape of corsets—and finally discarding them altogether in favor of a more natural look. The female silhouette during this period of fashion changed from a molded hip with bell-flared skirts to a straight chemise or slip-style dress that climbed right to the knee by 1925. Chanel and Vionnet, both French designers, greatly favored the looser styles, and their corsetless clothing caused a sensation. The corset was replaced by a soft girdle; breasts were held firm by a soft bandeau or camisole. A new and more boyish figure was in the making, with little resemblance to the lady of Victorian England. The permanent wave was invented, women hennaed their hair, and visible makeup became acceptable.

1920–1930: A Short Decade

The postwar look for men included worsted or flannel suits with uncuffed trousers and a waistcoat or vest; a black dinner jacket, worn with a silk bowtie; and a single-breasted chesterfield coat, usually in midnight blue. The waterproof trench coat continued to be the major military influence on day dress.

Voluminous knickers appeared—wools for winter, white linen for summer—and the men's summer suit in heavy linen or shantung was worn for business from Florida to Massachusetts. A raccoon coat was appropriate winter equipment for football games and open cars. In the fifties these coats became great gear for so-called flapper parties, and again in the seventies they were briefly back in style.

Women's dressing, on the other hand, had great variety, and it seemed that changes were occurring every two years. During the twenties skirts went from ankle length for day clothes in 1921 to very short by 1925, when they reached the knee. Never before in the history of fashion did a woman wear a skirt so short. Skirts stayed short for a couple of years and then began their inevitable descent. By 1930 all evening dresses touched the ground and day dresses were midcalf.

A one-piece foundation garment was de rigueur in the twenties. Hardly a slip could be found in the land except under a transparent dress or gown. The silhouette was straight, with the belt low on the hip. In the last years of the decade, the waist rose up to its normal position as hemlines went down.

Beaded clothing was in fashion for day and evening; synthetic velvets and silks became à la mode for French designers. Standard day wear for many women was the little black (or navy) dress with a matching coat.

Head shapes got smaller during the twenties as hair was bobbed, and brimmed hats shrunk into

Left: *A 1925 afternoon flapper-style dress at its shortest, simply accessorized with cloche hat and pumps.* Below: *A 1920s evening gown fashioned with glittering beads and an uneven hemline.*

Three distinct and classic looks for women of the thirties and forties, left to right: The casual daytime sportiness of pleated trousers; the classic 1930s Coco Chanel suit worn by the designer and impeccably accessorized with kid gloves, pearl strands, and head-hugging hat; the elegant bias-cut, silver-woven evening dress worn by Carole Lombard.

the small fitted cloches. Brilliant-colored silk pajamas made their appearance in the bedroom—and on the beach. Suntans came into vogue.

Horseback riding and skiing put sports-minded women in trousers in the twenties and paved the way for more mannish daytime clothing by the 1930s.

1930–1942: Hollywood . . . and War

While Englishmen demand custom-made clothing, American menswear designers have always searched for a real American ready-made, sportier style. Yet with few exceptions, they still followed London's lead in tailoring and style.

After years of the classic dark blue suit, we be-

gan to see suits in blue-green, pinkish beige, and brighter blues. Patterns such as herringbone, pinstripe, and checks were favorites for suits. And for a sportier look, Harris tweeds in heather colors enjoyed great demand. Jacket linings were largely synthetic instead of silk.

A popular sporty shoe was the slipper-style moccasin often worn with pleated pants; short-sleeved shirts were "invented" for golf and country outings. Hollywood movie directors made this casual yet sophisticated style their own, and it was immediately copied by men all over America.

By 1942, England and the United States had to conserve materials for the armed forces, and the "utility suit" of synthetic fabric, few buttons, and narrow-cuffed trousers was born.

Yet with all of these minor changes and variations in lapels, buttons, and trouser widths, one can still look at a single- or double breasted suit from 1905 or 1940 and see a similar line, fit, and style. The same goes for men's basic formal evening attire, from the black tailcoat right down to the patent-leather pumps.

As Hollywood began to influence men's clothing, it also influenced women's styles. Many fashion watchers believe that Mae West's portrayal of the title character in *Diamond Lil*, which was set in the 1890s, paved the way for the return of a voluptuous, fitted silhouette, which eventually peaked again in the late forties and early fifties.

During the thirties and forties, a slim, straight line alternated with a revival of Victorian touches like leg-o'-mutton sleeves, fitted bodices, and the suggestion of a bustle. The exaggerated square-shoulder silhouette arrived in 1933 and disappeared with the New Look in 1947.

The waist and bust remained in a normal position until 1938, when a boned corset that pulled in waists and thrust out the bust came back into fashion. And hems once again fluctuated: They were eight inches off the ground in 1931 and mid-calf length in 1940.

Very tailored clothes for town remained popular; and women imitated men's dinner suits by wearing white jackets, black skirts, and white blouses. Skiing and skating clothes had a manly look with pants and jackets in navy and black.

Costume jewelry in gold and silver with semi-precious stones and large handbags were in vogue.

Left: *Robert Montgomery and Clark Gable show off their late-forties riding outfits on the studio lot: jodhpurs, riding boots, sport jackets, and scarves.* Right: *Mae West paved the way for the return of the hourglass figure in such movies as* Diamond Lil *and* Klondike Annie.

All well-dressed women wore plenty of cosmetics and fingernail polish in colors from pale pink to brownish red.

1947: The "New Look" Takes Hold

The postwar look was influenced by the trend to more fitted waists and fuller skirts that began before the war and signaled a return to the hourglass figure—there was hardly a straight or slim hip line to be found. This determinedly female look was brought to the fashion world via Paris by Christian Dior. And although it was called the "New Look," there was—as we look at the history of fashion—very little about it that was new.

Keep in mind that the New Look was a reaction to slimness and the minimal use of fabric during the war effort. In any case, fashion is never static, and the industry is kept alive by a need for change. Going from narrow to wide and from long to short and vice versa every few years is the name of the game. Some styles became classics; some last a few years and die.

Aside from the stimulus the New Look afforded the fashion industry, it was a boon to women with bosoms and hips—Dior's wide circular skirt camouflaged them. And a fashionable woman couldn't wear a huge circular skirt without petticoats, so back came the crinoline, the stiffened petticoat of yesterday.

Ballet-length cocktail dresses, chic little hats, sheer nylon stockings with colored leather pumps, pouch or box bags, and scarves galore accessorized the postwar style. No one really got used to all those wartime synthetics, and so elegant fabrics, such as wool, broadcloth, rare fleeces, handwoven cottons, and silk velvets returned as soon as they could be manufactured.

It's hard for us to realize how little civilian manufacturing went on during the war; it took two years for production to return to normal. During wartime men could not get their favorite white cotton for shirts or wool for jackets, and so they wore bright-colored synthetic fabrics. By 1947 scarcity had created a new look for men. Gabardine trousers still had pleats, but rayon or silk shirts were brightly patterned and some jackets were two-toned.

Double-breasted overcoats were favored over

Postwar fashion received a jolt from Dior's 1947 Paris collection. Typical of the "New Look" is this Dior outfit, with its pinched-in waist, full skirt, padded-hip jacket, and high heels—a return to a very feminine look not seen during the war years.

single-breasted ones, as were double-breasted dinner jackets. Ski sweaters, moccasins or loafers, suede battle jackets, and ranch outfits with riding boots also became very popular with men. Gaily patterned scarves of silk, wool, or synthetics with contrasting colors became popular.

A more casual and comfortable lifestyle was on the rise in America as the fifties approached. And with it came the need for less formal clothing for both men and women.

The 1950s: Classics Become the Fashion

From the beginning of the twentieth century, a cult of conservative dressing based on the traditional elegance of London tailoring grew up among gentlemen from the Ivy League schools. In the fifties that style developed into a dress code for all businessmen. The Ivy League dresser wore slim trousers, narrow lapels, and natural shoulders with no padding. He wouldn't be caught dead in a hand-painted tie.

The modern American flair for casual smartness was evident in all the 1950s sportswear, as seen in the shorts or slacks for casual wear, beach, or golf. The sports shirt and jacket topped off this tropical look. Although the white shirt held its

own, especially for bankers, colored shirts were preferred by many professional men. And sports shirts were filled with colors, checks, and plaids.

We can't finish an account of the classics of the fifties without mentioning the gray flannel suit—that uniform worn by every business executive. And the Dacron-and-cotton drip-dry suit—no pressing required!

Certain classics took their place in a woman's wardrobe as well in the fifties; namely, the shirtdress and the shift or chemise. These styles—the first taken from the 1890s Gibson Girl, the second from the 1920s straight chemise shape—have never lost their fashion influence. They have been varied, shortened, and lengthened, but they remain in style. Shirtdressing opened the doors for classically styled shirts, first brought out by Brooks Brothers, for women. And the chemise dress led the way to T-shirt dresses. Women were looking not only for more casual clothes but for less frilly ones as well.

But that was only one 1950s direction. Chanel returned to the fashion scene with a short-jacketed suit and silk printed blouse that was an instant success. Sweaters took on a new dimension with chiffon linings and beaded or ribbon embroidery. Women tucked away their casual day wear

Marlon Brando and friends in The Wild One *exemplified one special look of the fifties.*

after five o'clock and showed up at parties in Oriental sheaths, harem pants, layers of chiffon, brocades, and shantung. And as a covering for these splendid fabrics, mink had very little competition. In the late 1950s, long-haired furs, such as fox and lynx, also became popular.

There's not much reason to talk about man-made fibers until the 1950s. For thousands of years, man has been happy weaving natural yarns: wool, linen, cotton, and silk. After World War II, there was an increase in yarns from laboratories; and they were woven into fabrics such as nylon, Orlon, acetate, and Dacron. They offered lower cost, lighter weight, and easier care—they could be washed or dry-cleaned. But as wonderful as man-made fibers were, natural fibers held their own in fashion.

The stretchable yarns used for undergarments seemed like a miracle to many women. The modern version of a corset is a glove-fitting nylon elastic, a far cry from the grim stays and bones of previous decades.

1960s: Short, Shorter, Shortest

If fashion watchers thought 1925 was the year of the short skirts, how did they deal with the minis of 1967? Along with short skirts came plastic go-go boots, white lipstick, and teased hair—a sort of pop, comic-book look. And jewelry was plastic, plastic, plastic.

If you had great gams you were in luck. And if you didn't, you prayed for the inevitable: a fashion reversal. And, of course, it came—first in flowing hippie-style long skirts, then with the high-fashion midi in 1971.

There was a lot of resistance to the hard, brassy mini-look. One fashion reaction: The appearance of vintage-clothing boutiques in the late 1960s. These shops expressed the need for options in the fashion marketplace. Since then the direction has been more and more toward individual style, hand-crafted pieces, and the mixing of the old with the new.

The great paradox of fashion is that although its very essence is change—wearing the *latest* thing makes you the *most* fashionable—a look at the past proves that all this movement is, as often as not, one step forward and two steps back. Styles

Brigitte Bardot in the briefest of minis and boots, 1966.

return as regularly as they disappear, like planets orbiting the sun. And often the most radical-looking fashions are inspired by a historical garment. The Romans copied the Greeks, the Restoration imitated the Renaissance, the forties stole from the Victorians, and the late seventies copied the forties. At least someone had the sense to call that the "retro" look.

The lesson for us is clear: Don't throw anything out! Well, not everything, but save clothes of good quality, no matter how strongly you feel that no one would ever, ever wear such a silly-looking thing again. They will, they will.

3

Shopping in a Vintage- Clothing Store

Vintage-clothing stores can seem intimidating, chaotic, and frustrating—until you learn the system. Discovering the best way of shopping in these stores is a challenge, and a worthwhile one. Shopping the vintage route is not like shopping in a department store, where there are fifty pieces of the same style in five colors and all sizes. (Now, that's chaos!) You can't learn everything on a one-day shopping spree. Some of the tips in this chapter will take time to learn; some will be quick and easy, like an old-fashioned Easter egg hunt.

"Eyeballing": Stock, Display, Organization

Organized shops are easier for the beginning shopper, so learn the ropes in these stores first. Men's and women's clothing will be hung separately and then grouped according to type and sometimes size. For example, Hawaiian shirts will be separated from gabardine shirts; tweed jackets from pleated pants. Women's blouses, dresses, and lingerie will be hung in groups if the shop has enough stock to form a group. If not, the item, such as a beaded dress, will be one of a kind. There should be a selection of clothes groups and a variety of sizes and colors.

In addition to the price, some shops have lots of information on their tickets, such as age of garment, size, and condition. I am always wary of a no-ticket, no-price system. This does not seem to be a fair way to run a clothing store. Most stores have dressing rooms. Always try on clothing for best results.

So far this seems easy. But learning how to make a selection among twenty-five gabardine shirts, each of which will be somewhat different in style, size, color, and condition, takes getting used to. The challenge—and the excitement—is in finding the one for you. Your own taste and personal style come into play. (Details about individual pieces of clothing and how to select them will be discussed in the chapters to come.)

Less organized shops with no orderly arrangement require more concentration and energy. Make up your mind that somewhere in this chaotic room is a blouse, coat, or scarf for you. If you do, then the fun begins. These are the kinds of stores that have always challenged me. Overachievers will feel their adrenaline level rising.

On your first shopping trips, you will probably look at everything, then only at colors you like and sizes that are right for your body. Finally, your hand will act like a Geiger counter. It will pass over the racks, touching only those items that are right for you. This takes training and time. Some customers claim to have X-ray vision as well as Geiger-counter hands. They can stand at the front door of a store and know if it is worth going in.

You'd be surprised how many shoppers panic and rip through the wire hangers. A calm approach is important; otherwise you will not see selections clearly. By the time you get home and gaze at your impulse purchase you'll realize that even if the color is perfect, it's just not your size. In these less organized stores, if there is no dressing room, try on clothing anywhere, but try it on.

Changes in stock can occur every day because clothes are coming in from many sources. There's always something new to look at. A lot of customers check in at their favorite stores regularly to catch the changing display of the history of fashion—and to make sure they don't miss anything.

Many shops try to have clothing in perfect condition, but this is difficult because competition for the best vintage clothes is so fierce. Check for a condition that satisfies you; relate that to a price you're willing to pay.

Left: *A well-organized vintage-clothing shop (such as this one, my store in New York City) has good visual display, well-placed mirrors and lighting, and clothing neatly organized by type.*

Is the Price Right?

How can you evaluate the value of vintage clothing in stores? After all, the clothing isn't being made today and priced according to hourly union wages and today's fabric costs. And what if you buy in a more expensive vintage-clothing store rather than a thrift shop or a flea market?

The great advantage of an organized store specializing in vintage clothing is that the owner has traveled for weeks, shopped for days, chosen, cleaned, and repaired what you are looking at. This is the edited and displayed version. The junk has been discarded. You are not digging through six large baskets at a thrift shop or flea market hoping to find one white-lace hanky. Flea markets and thrift shops in areas that are sophisticated

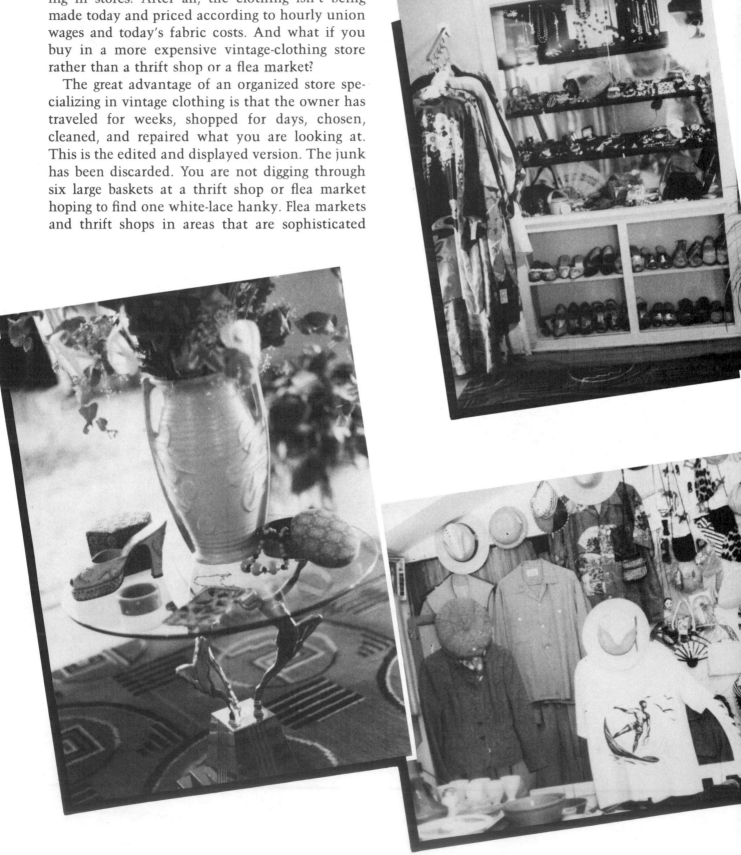

about fashion are often so picked over that finding a fabulous item for a pittance is like hunting for a truffle. Bargains and unrecognized treasures do exist, of course, but that takes time. More on how to find them later.

But it's not just a matter of letting the store owner do the hunting. The big difference is that vintage retailers get most of their stock from private sources that are not available to the public. Shop owners have multitudes of mysterious contacts. One winter, I bought a vintage collection stored in the trunk of a car that was parked at a restaurant on the Connecticut Turnpike because my source didn't want me to see her house. She said it was a mess. By the time I finished handling fabric, checking sizes, chatting, and purchasing, my hands were so cold I couldn't hold on to the steering wheel of my car.

Stores that edit charge for their talent, taste, and expertise, and most of the time it's worth it. The challenge and fun of finding a special item is still present, but it takes much less time. So the price is bound to be higher.

There are some interesting idiosyncrasies in pricing. The difference between prices in well-displayed, tasteful, service-oriented stores and those with six racks, 200 wire hangers, and a mir-

ror may not be as great as the consumer thinks. Often, it's just a few dollars. Also, the difference between flea market and store pricing is narrowing dramatically. In the latter, you have the advantages of dressing rooms, returns or exchanges, and service.

Sizing: Numbers, Numbers, Numbers

Sizing is another problem. Sizes marked on the insides of old clothing are as old-fashioned as the clothing itself.

Sizing of blouses was often related to bust measurements: 32, 34, 36, 38, which today correspond to 6, 8, 10, 12. Forty years ago, shoes were often hand-made and there were four widths to choose from: A, B, C, D. Hats were measured by the number of inches around the head. Socks were not labeled "one size fits all," but 9, 9½, 10, and so on. Dresses were sometimes custom-made, so no hint of a size can be found on the inside label. You can understand why I always feel lucky when I find a customer who fits perfectly into a custom-made vintage dress. To me it's like making the right match for a marriage.

As you can already see, it takes some adjustment and patience when trying on vintage clothes. Don't despair. Your ability to evaluate a garment's size will develop as you shop and try on vintage clothes.

One of the best ways to judge size is to examine three areas: shoulders, waist size, and hip room. Choose jackets and blouses for trying on based on your judgment of their shoulder width. Hold the garment up to you or ask the store owner to measure the shoulder line against your back. For dresses: Check shoulder and waist sizes first; then see if there is enough hip room. Hold the dress from side seam to side seam against your own waist. Do the same with pants and skirts. But no sucking in of the stomach! Until you become more accustomed to vintage clothing, ask questions concerning size; for example, "Have you seen this on? Is the waist as small as it seems?" This will also help prevent tearing already fragile garments, such as beaded chiffons and delicate batiste dresses.

Fabric and Style

You don't have to be a connoisseur to be able to enjoy shopping for vintage clothing. You will soon become familiar with the typical fabrics and styles of each period and be able to distinguish between silk and rayon as easily as you can spot the typical bias cutting of the thirties.

The first "landmarks" you'll learn to recognize will be the white cottons and linens of Victorian and Edwardian clothing. These dresses, blouses, and nightgowns made so much use of soft lawn and nubby linen that it's hard to confuse them with clothing of any other period.

After you've seen several peach silk nightgowns or teddies, you'll recognize peach as a favorite lingerie color of the twenties and thirties.

Print dresses of the 1940s were made in almost every conceivable color, but most often the background colors were black, navy, and brown; seldom will you find a dress with a green or burgundy background. And the prints used on these backgrounds will also become familiar: pink-and-green flower baskets, umbrellas, ballerinas, Scotty dogs, ladies' faces, and bold flowers.

Among the signposts of cut and style that you'll encounter is the use of the bias cut in dresses and nightgowns in the 1930s. Anyone who remembers the dresses Ginger Rogers wore when she was dancing with Fred Astaire has seen the most beautiful and dramatic examples of these elegant evening dresses.

After your first introduction, you'll never miss recognizing the padded shoulders of 1940s suit jackets. This exaggerated style made waists look smaller, hips narrower, and legs longer. And they were made in gabardine so often that you will never again wonder what gabardine looks like.

The musical *Grease* reminded us that circle skirts originated in the 1950s. Many shops specialize in fashions of the fifties, which are, of course, the inspiration for punk and new wave styles.

Vintage clothing provides a look into the future through the past. Everything being designed today was influenced by these earlier clothes. In vintage stores you see the best of this kind of clothing gathered together, accessorized—and probably worn by the owner. Of course, you don't have to be able to date a garment to love it and wear it. Some people simply enjoy knowing when things were made. The history is just part of the fun.

Pet Peeves of the Shop Owner

Allow me to make a few suggestions that will help you avoid hassles for the shop owner—and for yourself.

· Leave irritable mates and critical friends home. Learn to go by your own intuition and your own opinions of how you want to look. No one can see you as you see yourself.
· Don't put yourself down at every available moment. "Boy, am I ugly today—and short."
· Keep your story of the two-dollar silk blouse you found in a flea market in Indiana to yourself. Every vintage-clothes sales person has heard it.
· Ditto the story about the fabulous old clothes you found in your attic and threw out.
· Antique clothing can be fragile. Try on your correct size or ask for help.
· Don't shop with your dog or drag along your two toddlers.
· Bright red lipstick stains light-colored clothing. Take special care!

4

Flea-Market Shopping

Ten years ago I was visiting Atlantic City, my hometown, for a week. To break my daily vacation routine of beach-shower-barbecue-sleep, I planned one of many flea-market outings. There was no better companion than an old high-school friend, who was also beach- and child-weary. Someone handed me a giveaway antiques newspaper from a large, well-known market in Pennsylvania. I looked for the nearest location to Atlantic City and an ad large enough to be worth the trip. One full-page announcement struck my eye. "One hundred dealers of collectibles and antiques only—no junk—Saturday, August 28, from 10:00 A.M. to 6:00 P.M., St. Mary's Church, Pylesville, Maryland. Don't miss this one: Come early."

We decided that Pylesville couldn't be more than about two hours away, and since my friend was driving, I was enthusiastic. I had driven so much searching for Edwardian white lingerie that July that my eyes became crossed whenever I saw a white road line.

It was 80 degrees and sunny when we left, 94 degrees when we found Pylesville three hours later. Hope still fueled us. St. Mary's and the one hundred dealers should be easy to find: Look for lots of cars near a white steeple. We pulled up to a small turn-of-the-century church, a simple and charming setting, with people eating sandwiches and selling cookies and cakes on the lawn. Hope dwindled.

"Could you direct us to St. Mary's and the big flea market?" A teenager snickered and continued to eat his sponge cake. "This is it," someone said. I think it was the minister. Somewhere in Pylesville on a little church lawn, hope died. My friend Carol and I fell to our knees as if to pray. Actually we were hysterical. Ripples of laughter filled our throats and tears came to our eyes as we looked at the three tables of "merchandise." Cakes, Avon bottles, old books. Three hours of sweating and planning strategy; we had almost brought a walkie-talkie in order to cover all one hundred dealers.

The point: There are never any guarantees with flea markets and always a few surprises. Unfortunately, finding a solid-gold pin in a 50-cent basket happens too infrequently. Flea markets can be a mishmash of junk—or gems—found in an old attic. Sellers can be knowledgeable with fair prices or inexperienced and expensive. How do you become familiar with what is where and who is best to buy from? Flea markets are held at varying times in varying places. Some flea markets have discount tickets telling dates and places for others in the area. Local and national newspapers and collectors' magazines include announcements of flea markets and antique shows. Libraries, churches, schools, parking lots, coliseums, and fairgrounds devote a day or a week to either outdoor markets or fancier indoor antique shows. There is a section of Friday's *New York Times* devoted to listings and advertisements of shows. Informative articles on collectibles, such as clothing, have often been included along with announcements of clothing auctions. When deciding on flea markets to explore, stay in your local area first unless you are familiar with markets that have a reputation for selling good vintage clothing on a regular basis. If you want to try a large market that shows once a year, check with other people who have visited it before setting out on a three-hour trip.

Most flea markets that house dealers on a regular basis—for example, every Saturday and Sunday—and have been in business for years have something to show for it. They may not be as cheap as they were ten years ago and the merchandise may not be as old, but they are worth a visit. One of the largest and most famous in California is the Rose Bowl in Pasadena, with hundreds of dealers—and thousands of buyers—arriving as early as 6:00 A.M. In the East there is a flea market that is held three times a year—spring, summer, fall—in Brimfield, Massachusetts. This used to be one of my favorite shopping haunts. But two years ago another clothing dealer attacked my foot with her boot, trying to reach a silk robe before I did. After that I gave up on Brimfield.

Anything can happen at a flea market. Shopping at one can be as exciting as the hunt at dawn, or it can drag on and on all day without a single worthwhile purchase. I had been planning a special trip to the Friendship, Indiana, flea market in 1968. Before going there I stopped to visit in Washington, D.C., where I had an automobile accident. My knee and leg were injured, but I was undaunted. I arrived at the airport on a stretcher, and Eastern Airlines took me onto the plane to Indiana in a wheelchair. At the flea market I entered free, because the ticket taker couldn't bear to charge a person in a wheelchair $1.50. I arrived in New York on crutches, with a wheelchair and torn knee ligaments—plus five duffel bags filled with clothes for the store. And a big smile. (This kind of obsessiveness is not advised for the average buyer!)

So many people have complained to me over the years that they can never find anything at large marketplaces. They get dizzy looking at everything and usually go home empty-handed and with a headache. This is definitely because they are trying to look at everything and it overwhelms them. One friend confessed that she got seasick at large markets and couldn't focus her eyes by the end of the day.

Make up your mind before you start out that you can't look at everything. If you are determined to find a great evening purse and a lovely white nightgown, concentrate only on these two items while visiting the market. Train your eye to look at every beaded, silver, mesh, leather, and sequined purse at every stall. Keep away from everything else. If you don't spot nightgowns or purses at particular stalls, ask dealers if they have anything tucked away.

If you want a silver bracelet, skip booths without jewelry. It's a special kind of discipline. It may sound as if you're limiting yourself, but it does work.

When you're in the market for clothing, you have to be willing to look through everything that appears in reasonable condition. Much of it will be undesirable, and close scrutiny is required. When you are outside you have the advantage of

Right: *Bargains can still be found at rural and urban flea markets, where merchandise varies from recently made junk to perfect-condition gems.*

daylight; size is always a problem when there are no dressing rooms, and holding something up to you may not be sufficient. Finding coats, scarves, furs, hats, and other accessories is easy; but finding blouses and dresses in the right size is difficult. After some experience of looking at a lot of antique clothing at boutiques, you may learn to gauge the shoulder and waist size by eye. In many older styles, the hip area is slightly gathered, so you have leeway there. Check underarms carefully, and look for tears in fabrics (as opposed to separated seams, which are easily repaired). Remember to check the length of a dress; hold it at the waist rather than at the shoulder. Look to see if there is an extrawide hem so that you can let it down if necessary. If you see a suit that you like at a market, try on the jacket and hold the skirt to your waist, keeping in mind the hip room in a straight skirt. When buying shoes, furs, or silk lingerie at flea markets, remember one important fact: It is almost never returnable. It's a one-shot deal—unless the seller also has a shop or agrees to let you bring it back the next weekend. So buy carefully or buy cheap.

A few tips before we get to the subject of prices:

· If you find a flea market that's open every weekend, the possibility of finding good merchandise increases with the number of visits you make, because you become familiar with the clothing dealers; they treat you as a repeat customer. They may even find special items for you if you get to know them well.
· Become familiar with the taste of each dealer

and the condition of the clothing they buy. Most clothing dealers at flea markets buy in private houses in their local town. They will have clothes from areas you may never visit because of distance. They bring this fresh merchandise to the flea market each week. So the possibilities are endless.

· Get there early. If a flea market opens at 10:00 A.M., and you arrive at 4:00 P.M., you have only one advantage (especially on a rainy day): You can buy unsold merchandise from a desperate dealer—at good prices. I found a gorgeous alligator purse that way once. I arrived at the last minute at a Berkeley flea market as everyone was packing up. A dealer discovered that she had forgotten to put the alligator purse on her table. I saw her from another aisle, heard her wail, and snatched up the purse as soon as she exhibited it.

Pricing at flea markets can be very reasonable or ridiculously high. Dealers who are also shop owners often travel far to set up at a flea market and must consider travel expenses and time when pricing their items. I have sometimes paid more for a kimono or silk blouse at a market than I would have paid for it at a retail store. At one Sunday flea market I found clothing I had thrown out from my store because I couldn't sell it at any price. It had been washed and pressed and was selling like hotcakes. One person's discards are another person's fashion.

Bargaining is common at most flea markets. Some dealers give 10 percent off to anyone who asks for a break on more than one item. This satisfies a buyer's need to pay less than the retail price. Other sellers give discounts to people in the fashion trade who are going to resell the merchandise. And some reduce their prices greatly if the buyer takes a number of items.

Many dealers at flea markets complain that customers take advantage. They treat clothing and other fragile merchandise carelessly, and then they want it for less than it cost the dealer to buy

it. When an item is marked $35 and you ask for it to be reduced to $15, don't expect applause.

When bargaining you might say something like "Would you consider a small reduction on this Victorian nightgown?" Or, "Would you take less than forty dollars on these two pairs of shoes?" This is certainly better than saying, "I bought stuff like this in California by the dozens for five dollars, and you're asking thirty-five dollars." But bargaining is certainly possible if you are reasonable and *tactful*.

Another point about flea-market shopping—of *any* antique-clothes shopping—is to buy what no one else wants at the moment. If you're not quick enough to grab what is being most sought after (and, of course, you're competing with shop owners at flea markets), you can find possibilities in what is left over but still usable. This calls for a lot of imagination. For example: linen and lace tablecloths make great harem pants. Don't laugh. I've seen someone do this, and the finished look was beautiful. (She could sew, of course.)

Other things you can do with miscellaneous flea-market purchases:

· Beaded and embroidered fabric can be used in a half-dozen different ways. Use beaded dresses that are irreparable or odd pieces of beaded fabrics on a jacket pocket. . . . Make a belt or an evening bag. . . . Or use the beads to make your own jewelry or to sew on clothes.
· Linen dresser cloths with handmade lace can become blouse sleeves, camisoles, lingerie cases, or summer evening purses.
· Buy belts without buckles or buckles without

belts and look for the other part. It's cheaper that way.
· Turn unlined furs inside out, and cut off the sleeves. This makes a great vest with the fur worn inside, and the outside will look like leather patchwork.
· Old silk ribbon is good for trim, belts, and jewelry.
· Never pass up good buttons—carved wood, Deco or forties plastic, cast pewter, and so on. Many jackets, coats, and sweaters, new or old, look 100 percent better with great buttons.
· Interesting and colorful paper fans are wonderful ways to decorate your dresser and fun to carry on a summer night.
· Use torn or faded kimono sections as obis, vests, blouses, or sleeveless tunics.
· An eyelet or lace petticoat with rust stains can be salvaged if you learn to use dyes. Dye rust stains russet or purple, or try a product called Whink for rust removal.
· Christening gowns for babies are not very salable, so you might find a good bargain. The skirts are so full that you can cut off the top and use the bottom—with all the handwork—for an adult's gathered skirt. Make the waistband from colorful old ribbon.
· Damask tablecloths and napkins never sell well at flea markets, but cloths make great harem pants. Dyed napkins can be used as scarves. Make sure to get large ones.
· Buy the large, gaudy forties-style silver pins that no one seems to want. You can pick them up for very little money and wear them on hats and lapels or as belt or shoe buckles.

Left: *When shopping at flea markets, be aware of varying condition—check clothing and accessories carefully.*

$ 350.

5

Buying at Auction

Going to an auction is great entertainment, and vintage clothes are being auctioned off now along with other valuable collectibles. Just be sure *you* are having fun. You want to be like the happy woman who went home with three Chanel suits for the price of one—not the woman who bid wildly on a beaded dress, got it, wrote out a check, and ran all the way to her bank to cover it.

There are two types of auctions where you'll find clothing. The typical country auction sells the contents of one or more estates, many of which include clothing along with the furniture, household, and garage items. Ten or fifteen years ago, when clothes were sold by the box loads, you could hear auctioneers say "It looks like sixteen pieces of white underwear here. Somebody give me a dollar." And you could go home with a box of camisoles for about four dollars. Now, of course, auctioneers are more aware, and clothes tend to be sold individually or in pairs; usually a good dress is sold with one in bad condition. Country auctions are held from early spring until Christmas, even in cold climates; and even if you don't find something worth buying, it's a good excuse for a picnic.

If you live in or visit New York, check out the regular (four to six times a year) sales of antique clothing held by the prestigious auction houses Sotheby's and Christie's East, a division of Christie's. Other auction houses and galleries in New York and other cities have an occasional sale of antique clothing. If you get to London, you're really in luck. The antique-clothes market there is strong; the English never throw anything away and have a longer tradition of collecting vintage clothing. The Christie's South Kensington branch holds clothing sales weekly or more often. Don't be frightened away by the fine-art reputations of the big-name places: *Some* of the clothes sold there *are* for collectors only, and it's a great chance to see and touch museum-quality pieces; *but* there are plenty of wearable items for the average buyer at prices comparable to those at a shop.

Auctions are advertised in local papers and via mailers from the auction houses. Those in the Northeast are announced in *Antiques* and *The Arts Weekly*, published in Newtown, Connecticut 06470. A subscription is $15 per year. The announcement will say whether or not an auction has clothes and give a rough indication of the selection.

If you're not familiar with auctions, go to one or two and sit on your hands. No bidding until you get the hang of it. You need to know how the bidding works, observe the pace of the auctioneer, and get a feel for price ranges. Be careful to avoid the major danger for the new auction goer: impulsiveness. I can't tell you how many tales of woe I've heard from people whose enthusiasm in the exciting auction atmosphere got the better of their sound judgment. It's very easy to fall into the trap of overpaying or buying something you'll never look at again.

Number-One Rule: Look Before You Buy

The most important part of auction buying is the preview. Never, never bid on anything that you have not carefully examined. At country auctions the preview is usually short, an hour or two before the sale starts. The major auction houses print descriptive catalogs of the items to be offered, and there are usually several days of preview time. Read the catalog, if there is one, carefully; then examine the garment. Try to determine the condition of the fabric: The older the garment, the more important this is. Look for stains, tears, and repairs, and check the most common trouble spots: the armpit area, collar or neckline, buttons and buttonholes. There is no opportunity to try

Some of the kinds of beauties you may see at auctions: Above: a green silk-damask skirt, with embroidered white satin facings and trimmed with fur; below: a hand-embroidered Chinese silk shawl with hand-tied silk fringe; opposite: a 1920s yellow chiffon evening dress embroidered with crystal and charcoal gray beads.

A Fortuny tea gown with Venetian bead trim.

things on, except maybe a quick slip-on of a jacket; so measure yourself and your own clothes and then take a tape measure to the preview so that you can get a better idea about fit. Finally, take a quick peek at your choices right before the sale begins to make sure that something delicate hasn't been mauled by the preview or torn by metal hangers, or that a sneaky cheater hasn't switched the contents of assorted lots of underwear or ripped out the Paris label you were coveting.

What's Your Price?

Rule number two is to decide how much you are willing to pay for what you want and stick to that figure. It's nice to think about getting something at a steal—and sometimes you can—but there's nothing wrong with paying what a garment is worth. Don't try to figure that out by seeing how the bidding is going. If it's low, great. If you've previewed carefully, you'll know that there's nothing wrong with the item, it's just unpopular today and you're in luck. But usually the best and most wearable things will be somewhat in demand. And you may be bidding against someone who has decided, for some personal reason, to get that particular item at any price. Remember: Things you think may sell for a lot may also sell for a little. And vice versa. Auction bidding is totally unpredictable, and the prices may have no relation to an item's real value. So make decisions ahead of time. Of course, it helps to know what antique-clothing shops are charging for similar things and what auction prices have been. A little research is a good idea.

You can sometimes get a good deal at the tail end of a country auction, when most of the crowd has tired and gone home. But auctioneers know this fact of human nature, too, and put the good stuff up for auction during prime time.

The sale of out-of-context items—clothes at a furniture auction, for example, or clothes of a different period from that advertised—can work two ways. They can go at a cheap price, because the people who would ordinarily bid for them aren't there. Or they can also sell for outrageous prices, because a bidder who does not know what they are worth makes the mistaken assumption that

he or she has lucked into the situation I just described.

Vintage clothes usually bring their true market value at Christie's and Sotheby's because they have a number of sales and draw the most knowledgeable buyers. Their catalogs include price estimates, but an auction is a horse race; the price can very well be much lower—or much higher. Don't be discouraged if the prices seem high at one sale; they could be half that at another.

Learn the Bidding Procedure

Before the auction starts, find out the ground rules. You may have to register and get a numbered paddle with which to bid. Ask about bidding increments. Bids often go up in $5, $10, or even $25 steps. Remember that, except in very unusual circumstances, you are buying "as is"; there are no returns. Country auctions are cash and carry, so bring money. Find out ahead of time if other places will accept checks or traveler's checks or cash only. Some big auction houses charge a 10 percent premium over the successful bid price. They also charge sales tax. Inquire about leaving a bid if you cannot attend a sale.

Avoid "Auction Fever"

When you bid, make your signal clear, and pay attention so that you don't bid on the wrong lot (if you do, tell the auctioneer *immediately*) or against your friend or even yourself. Strange things can sometimes happen because auctions go so fast. *Never* go above the dollar limit you set. Auction bidding is like gambling; if you are compulsive, stay away. Impulse buyers are better off at cosmetics counters where they won't lose the rent!

Beware of the country auctioneer's "patter." He is trying to drive the price up and may start by mentioning the price he hopes eventually to get.

Most important, try not to develop a proprietary feeling about something you liked at a preview. It may stimulate a competitiveness that will keep you bidding up and up. You'll get some things; you'll lose others. It's not a competition; you're not winning anything, you're paying for it. So don't get too excited.

The record holder for the highest price paid at an auction—a violet-and-ivory silk evening dress designed by Paul Poiret for his wife, which sold for $5,500 in May 1981 at Christie's East.

What to Look For

Most buyers at clothing auctions are young women looking for interesting clothes. The rest are dealers and store owners (although the latter depend mostly on private sources), serious costume collectors, and museum curators. Unless you are a fairly stylized dresser who wears Victorian bodices every day, you probably won't be interested in anything earlier than Edwardian. The white dresses, blouses, and lingerie of that period are so popular that you can't expect a bargain. Prices are high, but remember that if the dealer next to you buys it, the price will double in his or her store. If you are familiar with current prices, you'll know what's a good deal and avoid the situation in which two people want a particular dress and bid it way up.

It's the ever-increasing Fortuny prices and twentieth century couturiers that get the publicity and scare people off. Yet Sotheby's will continue to devote itself exclusively to this quality and price range as of 1982. Christie's East's most recent average lot prices were $150 and up, so there are few possibilities for the average buyer.

Collectors keep an eye out for anything that is really a good example of its period and for early, innovative clothes by well-known designers. Some collectors concentrate on one type of item, a period, or a designer. Certain designers are considered highly collectible, especially Mario Fortuny, whose unique pleated evening dresses are fetching thousands of dollars. Aficionados hunt for beaded dresses by Callot Soeurs, evening clothes by Lanvin, Poiret, and Vionnet, and early Chanel designs. Sometimes collectors try to anticipate the market by buying later designer labels like Givenchy, Balmain, Galanos, Charles James, Adrian, and Claire McCardell.

You should look for only what you like unless you are a collector. Clothes *are* an "investment," and although they are a fragile collectible there is a growing audience that finds them valuable. Furthermore, you have to be an expert to judge whether a designer garment is genuine. Label switching and misrepresentation on labels are not uncommon, and the connoisseurship of even the most reputable places is not infallible. Don't pay more than what a garment is worth to you as something to wear.

My advice is forget labels, and go for the styles you like. Day clothes tend to be cheaper than evening dresses; plain things are overlooked in favor of flash. An exquisite and eye-catching beaded-chiffon evening blouse, dated about 1930, can be worth a price of $150 when you think that department stores sell high-quality but anonymous-looking silk blouses for more than that. Except for museum-quality things, nineteenth-century clothes usually go for low prices.

The ideal buyer, according to some country auctioneers, is the one who can see the creative possibilities in a dress with a ruined skirt and know how to turn it into a blouse. Or how to enlarge a small nineteenth-century top using the material from a hem. Clothes from the twenties and before are rarely in perfect condition. But the hand finishing and embroidery on clothes of that period will never be done again.

Whether you buy imperfect twenties dresses for their hand embroidery or bid successfully on a perfect-condition Adrian forties suit, you'll find auctions a fascinating mixed bag of treasures, challenges—and some schlock. Good luck!

PRICES

Here's roughly the range you can expect to pay for clothing at auctions. These prices reflect 1981 and early 1982 averages and depend on condition, style, and date of garment.

Beaded 1920s dresses: $40–$700
White lingerie dress from 1900: $60–$500
Dior ball gown from 1950s: $75–$100
White Edwardian blouse: $40–$175
Couturier dress or suit: $60–$600

6

Finding Your Own Sources

The Family

Resourceful vintage-clothing shoppers start in their own backyards or attics first. Don't take this suggestion too literally, of course, because vintage clothes aren't in the yard, nor do many people have attics these days. But older family members do have some wonderful surprises tucked away in drawers or buried in old gift boxes. I should know: Some of my first finds—hats, gloves, laces, and a 1920s coat—came from an eighty-nine-year-old friend of my mother's.

Ask aunts, uncles, grandmothers, neighbors, and your mother if they have saved anything nostalgic from their trousseau or wedding. That's a good place to begin. Many women have saved their wedding dresses, lace hankies, or special peignoirs. Uncles often saved their white-kid evening gloves or a silk opera scarf. Aunts and great-aunts always turn up a hand-beaded purse (usually with an old ticket stub still in it).

Travel

People never believe me when I tell them I've found vintage clothing and jewelry on almost every winter vacation I've taken to the Caribbean, Florida, or Mexico in the last ten years.

In the Caribbean I recently found old and never-worn Chinese embroidered blouses in a gift shop. The stock was from 1955, and when the new owner of the store took over, he emptied the basement and sold these blouses at their 1955 prices (very cheap).

Florida thrift shops in such places as Palm Beach, where wealthy people winter, were once known for their vintage-clothing bargains. Now pickings are slimmer but not altogether gone. On a recent visit I found these items in south Florida: a 1950s cashmere sweater, a pair of 1930s gold sandals, some very inexpensive silver pins, a 1940s linen blouse, and twelve old damask dinner napkins.

Mexico is well known for its silversmiths. Some very beautiful old hand-wrought silver jewelry can be found, but it takes searching out. Villages outside of Mexico City or other large cities may have 1940s and 1950s hand-painted, sequined skirts and blouses. Tijuana and southern California are two other vacation spots to check out for handmade Mexican finery (see store listings at back of book).

Now that it's not so unusual to travel to the Orient these days, let me remind you of the treasures you will find in Hong Kong, Peking, Kyoto, or Tokyo. It's important to ask for antique or old embroidered clothing; otherwise you will only be told of the newly manufactured things.

The large flea markets in Rome, Paris, and London all have sections devoted to vintage clothing. These are usually open on weekends only, so check locations and times beforehand. Ask your concierge if you can't get this information on your own.

Charity Sales, Museum Costume Sales, Churches, Historical Societies

Many churches, museums, and charities have yearly sales of vintage clothing or antiques to raise money. It may be worth your while to find out ahead of time when these sales will be held so that you can be first on line for buying. The things found at these sales have been donated by community members. The South and New England in particular are excellent sources for charity bazaars.

PART TWO

The Head-to-Toe Guide: What to Buy, How to Wear It

7

Lingerie: Pretty Innerwear, Pretty Outerwear

When I first opened my shop, I stocked lingerie—especially from the twenties and thirties—in abundance: lace-edged teddies, bare camisoles, slips, nightgowns, knitted bed jackets, and of course everything in silk. I can't remember putting a rayon nightgown in my shop until 1973. Blythe Danner, Kathleen Widdows, and Nancy Allen were regular customers, scouting for vintage lingerie they could wear as outerwear to parties and openings. Other customers bought the peach silk bed jackets on display for hospitalized friends instead of boxes of candy—silk lingerie was *very* inexpensive at that time. Whenever December rolls around, I remember one Christmas during my early years of selling vintage lingerie when Debbie Reynolds came in. She oohed and ahed over my collection of satins and silks and then snapped up every great piece of lingerie in the shop, along with some beaded dresses, while her chauffeur dutifully waited at the door to carry out the packages piling up in his arms. That is, until an overly inquisitive fan started questioning Debbie about her best performances, how she liked show business, and whether she was still friends with Donald O'Connor. Debbie's shopping spree abruptly ended.

Victorian and Edwardian "Whites"

White cotton lingerie from the late 1880s and early 1900s is among the most collectible antique clothing you'll find. Among these beauties are long, handmade nightdresses; bloomers and petticoats, usually with lace and eyelet ruffling; delicate laces and hand-embroidered camisoles (which were worn over the corset and also called corset covers); combing coats (worn to protect clothes and lingerie when combing hair); and chemises (worn as underslips). The styles vary from high-necked primness to low-cut romantic sexiness, and the pieces of lingerie are so beautiful

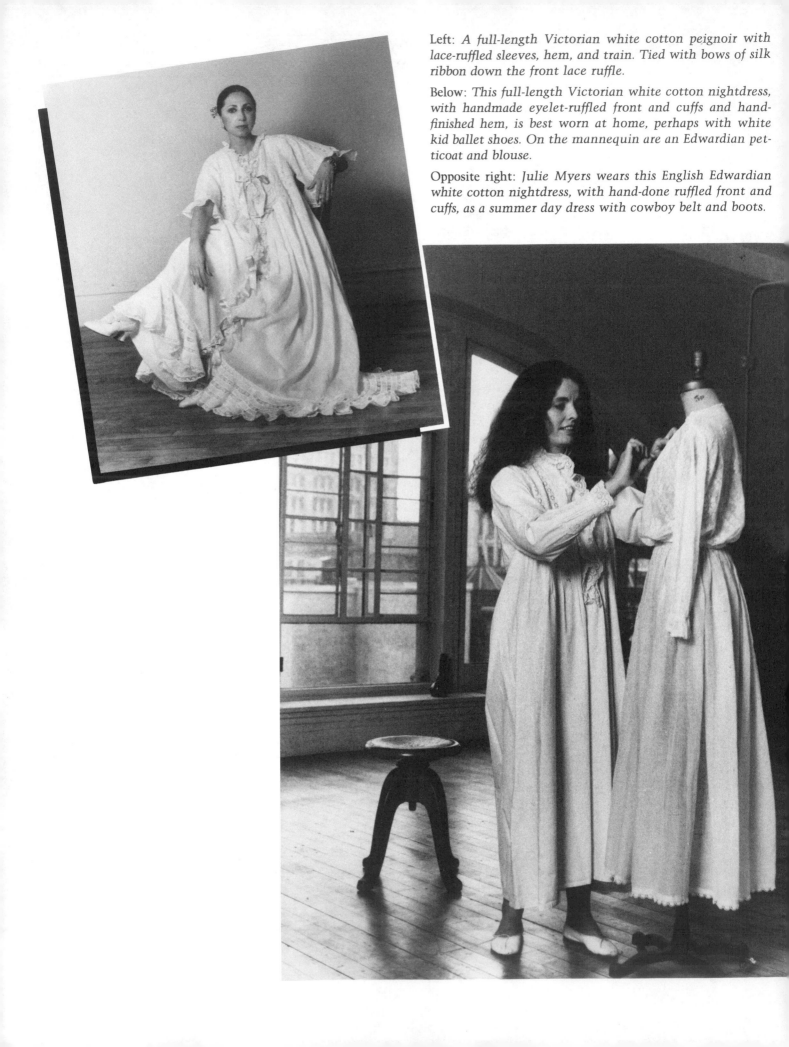

Left: *A full-length Victorian white cotton peignoir with lace-ruffled sleeves, hem, and train. Tied with bows of silk ribbon down the front lace ruffle.*

Below: *This full-length Victorian white cotton nightdress, with handmade eyelet-ruffled front and cuffs and hand-finished hem, is best worn at home, perhaps with white kid ballet shoes. On the mannequin are an Edwardian petticoat and blouse.*

Opposite right: *Julie Myers wears this English Edwardian white cotton nightdress, with hand-done ruffled front and cuffs, as a summer day dress with cowboy belt and boots.*

that it is hard to believe they were worn strictly as underwear. But they were. The wealthy women of Europe and America had as much masterful handwork put into their undergarments, especially their trousseaus, as they had put into their outerwear. Handmade lace, French seams, and hand-finished hems were commonplace. So were the personal maids employed to launder them.

Rich women were not the only ones to have beautifully made undergarments. In Catholic countries, such as France and Italy, the nuns not only hand-stitched their own undergarments but made their own broadcloth fabrics. They also made *grand-père* nightshirts for the priests. You can still find these simple but well-made garments if you travel the French countryside.

The best Victorian and Edwardian handmade white lingerie I ever bought for the shop was from London. I made a special trip there in the spring of 1973 to purchase a trousseau made for a British baroness in the late 1890s. I paid between $15 and $20 for each piece—all perfect examples of the most pristine night wear I had ever seen. Today they would cost ten times that much.

I first introduced Victorian and Edwardian whites into my store in 1969. Barbara Bersell, a photographer who was with *Vogue* magazine at the time, discovered this lingerie in my shop and featured it in *Vogue* on many occasions. Her "find" brought Edwardian lingerie into the public eye, and I began getting phone calls from all over the United States. Some of my fanciest Edwardian peignoirs were worn by customers as wedding dresses. Other whites were bought by mothers for their young daughters to wear to high-school graduation. Some of my smallest-size long batiste gowns with tiny waists served this purpose well.

The best examples of white lingerie are found in the more expensive antique-clothing boutiques in England, France, and the United States. The boutique owners who specialize in Edwardian whites have cornered the market, although on occasion good-quality whites can still be found at New York City auctions, flea markets, or house sales held in small cities. Many moderate-priced boutiques will carry a few pieces of Edwardian lingerie year-round. And if you're lucky you can find a white Victorian nightgown or camisole hanging in a country antique shop. If you do, grab

it. It can be a bargain purchase if the shop's specialty is not clothing.

HOW TO WEAR WHITES

If I had to choose one piece of white lingerie to buy, I would pick a handmade Victorian or Edwardian nightdress—with front pin tucking, hand-crocheted cuffs and collar, or handmade eyelet trim. I own three of these long nightdresses: one I wear for sleeping, the other two I wear as day dresses—open at the neck and belted. The kind of belt you choose "creates" the mood. A cowboy belt, paired with cowboy boots, makes the dress very casual. An Edwardian nightgown can also be teamed with a bright-colored crew-neck sweater or vest and a textured belt (such as lizard). Blouse the top slightly over the belt.

Lightweight nightdresses and hand-embroidered chemises make good beach cover-ups—a great way to wear a chemise that is too short to belt as a

Right and opposite: *Lace-edged knee-length bloomers make wonderful summer shorts or, paired with a waist-hugging camisole, a romantic "at home" outfit. The same camisole, teamed with a lovely crisp cotton 1915 petticoat, can be worn as a summer resort outfit. Below: Two ways to convert lingerie into outerwear. Phyllis Posnick (left) pairs a hand-embroidered linen chemise with a Moroccan silver belt for a cool summer look; and (right), a lace-trimmed cotton teddy with a drawstring tie at the waist and neck is loose enough to look like a short summer culotte on Sarah Fields.*

down" a petticoat with a striped T-shirt, a colorful, woven-cotton belt, and pastel tights. (If your petticoat has a drawstring, you might want to wear a belt to cover the string.)

Sleeveless white chemises or less dressy camisoles can be paired with brightly colored cotton pants. They can also be tucked into the petticoats or worn over them. Mixing white with bright colors—or keeping the look all white—gives Edwardian lingerie lots of versatility, lots of summer looks.

CARING FOR WHITES

Many people are not willing to spend the money or the time required to own vintage whites—and they're missing out on something special. Although vintage white lingerie requires special care (particularly if you want to wear it often), it's worth it. Here are some laundering hints I've picked up, all to make upkeep easier.

First, buy the best-condition garment possible for the price you can afford; keep it clean and covered on a padded hanger when you are not wearing it. Vintage white lingerie that has been hanging in your closet without wear for a year may begin to turn yellow. To whiten it, follow this mild recipe: 1½ gallons cold water—or enough water to cover your garment; 1 cup well-dissolved Snowy Bleach, Biz, or Clorox Two. To dissolve powdered bleach: use a small amount of very hot water. Soak your garment for an hour or two, depending on how yellow it has become. Check after one hour; if it has not whitened, let it soak longer. (Clorox Two, Biz, and Snowy are nonchlorine bleaches; their bleaching action, which is done with the ingredient sodium perborate, is mild and takes a little longer than using chlorine bleach.)

If a long soaking with the nonchlorine bleach does not work, follow this stronger recipe—it should work: 2 gallons warm water to cover garment; ½ cup liquid chlorine bleach. Liquid chlorine bleach can act very fast—so watch your garment carefully. It may turn white in only fifteen minutes. But if it does not, let the garment keep soaking. If, after a few hours, you need more bleaching action, change the water and add fresh liquid bleach. If that doesn't work, increase the

dress. Lace-edged bloomers make good summer "shorts," too, and they can be washed in the machine. Often they don't need to be ironed. If you find a long lace-edged pair that comes to the ankle, wear them during a summer evening with a T-shirt. Bloomers can be very baggy, so make sure you're comfortable with that look before venturing out.

Look for heavy-cotton petticoats trimmed with lace or crocheting. They make beautiful summer skirts. If you find one that is too long, shorten it *from the waistband* to save the handwork on the bottom. Turn the waistband over (folding under one-quarter of an inch for a finished edge); the band should be about one inch wide; cut off any extra fabric from the top. Add a drawstring to give you an adjustable waistband.

A petticoat can be worn with a white cotton camisole on a summer evening. A dressier lace camisole with a white petticoat can be the answer to an afternoon wedding or a garden party. "Dress

amount of bleach. But watch carefully to be sure you don't dissolve the entire garment.

When you cannot resist buying a petticoat or blouse that is practically brown when it should be white, you will need to give it even more "treatment." One of my customers soaked a dirty white cotton dressing gown for three weeks using liquid chlorine bleach, changing the water every day. She now has a lovely white dressing gown. But keep in mind: All bleaching—especially chlorine bleaching—strains and damages cotton fibers.

This final recipe should be kept for desperate measures. Do this in a washing machine on a soak-and-gentle-wash cycle:

Hot water
1 cup dishwasher detergent (Calgonite or any
 cheaper version)
½ cup liquid chlorine bleach
Soak for ¼ to 3 hours, then wash.

Use this bleaching recipe on sheets and pillowcases, too.

One note: Museums and costume institutes would never approve of these techniques for dealing with white cotton and linen garments, because they are in the business of preserving textiles. You, on the other hand, are trying to make something wearable, now.

Twenties and Thirties: Slinkier . . . Sexier

Innerwear of the twenties and thirties tended to resemble the styling of each decades' outerwear: Twenties lingerie and nightdresses were chemise straight with tie belts at the hip and often had the

Above: *This lovely 1930s peignoir of silk chiffon features smocked waist and wrists, covered buttons, and full sleeves.* Below: *Two rare black silk-chiffon nightgowns: one tied at the neck and waist and hand embroidered all over with pink birds; the other embroidered in pink, lilac, and white flowers and leaves. Both are completely handmade.* Opposite: *Carol Troy wears a full-length, bias-cut, ivory satin nightdress with long lace-edged sleeves, lace-trimmed V-neck, and satin train—a lovely dress for "at home" entertaining.*

Left: *Alexandra Penney's choice for a spring cover-up: yellow chenille robe over jeans and a man's shirt. An old square eyelet-linen napkin serves as a scarf.*

Below: *Originally made to be worn at home, bed jackets now work well over camisoles or as blouses. This short-sleeved, apricot-colored quilted satin jacket is worn over a satin nightgown with a paste necklace for evening.*

same detailing—pleating, shirring, yokes—as twenties dresses. Thirties lingerie was bias cut, more fitted and flowing, with fuller skirts, tighter bodices, and puffy sleeves.

Lingerie from the twenties and thirties are the clothes dreams are made of, the fashion we have all seen in dozens of late-night movies. Gorgeous silk teddies; lace-trimmed slips; bias-cut nighties, which never seem to go out of style; ribbon-tied panne-velvet bed jackets to the hip, with inches of lace in deep berry tones; and zippered satin robes with full sleeves that can't be hidden away in the closet or worn only in the bedroom anymore. Women are buying twenties and thirties lingerie to wear as evening dresses and gowns.

I have a lace-trimmed cream satin nightgown in my wardrobe that was originally made in 1932. There are no sleeves, only a lace cap falling softly over the shoulder. I wear it as a dress on special occasions—under a belted beige-silk pongee kimono printed with turquoise-and-melon flowers—and no one thinks I've just gotten out of bed!

Among the most collectible twenties pieces: a silk-chiffon or crepe chemise-style nightgown trimmed in handmade lace and sometimes monogrammed. Or a peach silk-jersey bra that slightly flattens the bosom, with matching peach jersey panties, often hand appliquéd on the leg with flowers or initials, the waist either elasticized or buttoning up the side, and the legs always full cut, imitating a panty skirt. Or the "boudoir" crepe de chine lounging pajama, in a range of wonderful colors. Speaking of colors, the silk lingerie of the twenties, thirties, and even forties had one characteristic in common: It all came in pale colors, such as soft pink, apricot, or peach—"bare" colors usually associated with a more private atmosphere.

Other sexy, sensational lingerie to look for: the camisole and the teddy (an all-in-one combination of bra and pants or slip). Often the bodice of the teddy was embroidered with flowers or initials, the edges trimmed in Cluny lace, with thin hand-stitched slip straps. Some of the prettiest have drawstrings at the waist or just under the bust, or both places. Teddies and camisoles work well under silk blouses, see-through clothes, or on their own as bare camisoles worn with an evening shirt, a lamé belt, and—in cooler weather—a shawl

or jacket. And their colorings are lovely: pale sherbets of lime, peach, apricot; sometimes a soft floral print; and, if you're lucky enough to find it, the rare black chiffon or satin, with pink or ecru lace trim.

Teddies were also popular in the thirties, as were form-fitting slips—alternatives to the teddy or to a bra and silk knickers.

The biggest "hits" of thirties clothing: the swirling bias-cut nightgowns and robes with clinging, revealing bodices, flowing skirts, and full sleeves made of silk satins with French-lace trim and straps. Putting on one of these gorgeous gowns makes you feel like Jean Harlow.

And from 1930s China came sleeveless bias-cut nightgowns, cut low in the back, with jacquard embroidered patterns and matching piped edges. I always feel lucky when I get one of these gowns, which must have been given as a gift from someone returning from mainland China. They are usually in mint condition and never cost less than $100.

Bed Jackets and Robes

Bed jackets were once for keeping you warm—and pretty—in bed. Now try a velvet or satin jacket as a blouse, over slim pants, or over men's silk pajama tops. If the sleeves are too long, roll them up. If the bed jacket is too big, blouse it over jeans or straight pants and belt it.

Quilted, chenille, wool, or rayon-satin robes don't have to be worn in front of the fireplace only. Many of my customers have purchased them as lightweight spring coats. Judith Van Amringe, a well-known accessories designer, bought a man's printed black-satin robe and wears it as an evening dress or coat. Alexandra Penney wears her red-bordered yellow-chenille robe with a large peacock on the back over jeans and a man's striped shirt. Substitute a thin lizard belt for the self-belt tassled tie, and voilà—you've got a dress instead of a robe. One note: Make sure the cuffed sleeves are not too long; roll them up or have them shortened by a tailor. Many printed-rayon robes from the forties work as dresses (but they must be shortened). Two companies that made thousands of these printed robes are Saybury and Textron. Their Deco and floral designs should never be

wasted in the bedroom! Removing the matching tie belt and substituting a leather or interesting fabric belt (in a solid color that works with the print) will convert the robe from lingerie into day wear.

Forties and Fifties Lingerie

In the forties and fifties, lingerie could be bought either in silk or rayon fabric (see Glossary). By the late fifties, rayon acetate became a popular and acceptable fiber. And although nothing is as wonderful against the skin as silk or cotton, the rayons and rayon acetates of the forties and fifties are almost as good and are abundantly available in shops and flea markets all over the United States. What to look for: forties and fifties dressing gowns or robes with padded shoulders or short puffy sleeves and full skirts in deep, dark tones—red, raspberry, teal, black, and cream. They look luxurious and they're wearable as dresses or as nightgowns—cheaper and sexier than almost any new garment you can find.

One note: If the top of the nightgown is in good condition but the bottom isn't, cut off the top and wear it as a blouse with jeans or printed pajama pants.

WASHING AND CARE OF SILK LINGERIE

Although I have had a lot of success washing old silk lingerie, many people have not. Fels Naphtha, which I think is the best cake soap, or Ivory soap—in liquid, flakes, or Snow—will work wonders on ordinary soil. The water does not have to be cold; tepid works fine. After washing silk lingerie, always press the garment on the wrong side to prevent iron marks; use steam.

Sometimes you find old lingerie that has never been worn. If it was in the attic wrapped in old tissue, it may be mildewed. Often a garment that has never been worn and has been in a damp place for many years is a worse purchase than a garment with a small tear, because the odors that develop from age and dampness do not wash out. The odor can sometimes be eliminated by a dry cleaner or by being aired in the sun. The risk in the case of dry cleaning is that the garment may fall apart—silk is very perishable. Keep this in mind.

Heavier-weight satin or flowing chiffon dressing gowns often have to be dry-cleaned, too. Hand pressing will stretch the satin and often lengthen the chiffon. A good dry cleaner who employs a good silk presser is hard to find these days. Your best bet: a dry cleaner with a cleaning plant on the premises.

Prices

Here's roughly what you can expect to pay for lingerie, depending on condition, style, and age.

White Victorian nightgown with hand-done eyelet and embroidery plus other hand-finished details: $150–$250

Other white embroidered nightgowns: $50–$100

Bloomers with handmade lace: $40–$90

Camisoles from simple machine-made versions to elaborate handmade ones with lace, ribbons, and embroidery: $55–$150

Short but decoratively embroidered chemise: $80–$150

1920s silk nightgown with lace: $60–$125

1930s silk or satin bias nightgown: $65–$150

Silk teddy with lace: $45–$90

Silk-velvet bed jacket: $50–$100

Printed rayon robe from the 1940s: $75–$90

Chenille or wool wrap robe: $40–$80

Man's striped or printed 1940s robe: $35–$85

1940s or 1950s rayon nightgowns and bed jackets: $25–$50

Carol Bovoso wears my ivory satin nightdress with lace trim under a kimono-style robe of slate blue pongee, embroidered with melon, gold, and cream-colored chrysanthemums.

8

Dresses: The All-in-One Fashion Basic

Many kinds of vintage clothing are popular, but none sell so consistently year after year as dresses. When I first went into the vintage-clothes business in 1965, I carried dresses almost exclusively. My racks were filled with everything from romantic, turn-of-the-century Edwardian and Victorian "whites," to body-skimming beaded evening dresses from the twenties, to silk-printed day dresses from the thirties and forties.

I'll bet you have a photograph of a relative wearing one of these late-afternoon thirties dresses, almost to the ankle, in soft-printed chiffon. My favorite photograph of thirties dressing is a picture of my mother, taken in a dress shop on the Atlantic City boardwalk in 1933, which I keep on the wall over my desk. My mother's hair is pulled back in a rolled bun, the hair fashion of the time, and she is wearing a midlength floral-printed chiffon dress with a cape (or "Bertha") collar, as she shops with friends, surrounded by racks of dresses from the thirties. The dresses are all very feminine, slightly frivolous . . . perfect, today, for a Sunday afternoon tea, for example, or for a cocktail party.

Vintage dresses really came into their own about fifteen years ago, when antique clothing began turning up at flea markets and private house sales. They were snapped up by women with original style and a special fashion sense, women who were looking for something unusual that would make a difference in the way they looked and dressed. Marisol, the New York artist and sculptor, was one of my first customers. She came to the shop regularly (and still does), searching for mandarin-style embroidered Chinese jackets (she collects these), beaded silk jackets, anything "evening," pizzazz-y, to wear over pants.

In the early days I would not only sell vintage dresses but lend them, too. But after one of my very special dresses, a multicolored lamé gown from the thirties, was "borrowed" by a well-known actress for a movie she was making in Italy and then returned to me tattered, six months later, I stopped lending my most valuable pieces and started renting them.

The real "boost" came when filmmakers and advertising agencies began renting turn-of-the-century "whites," clinging bias satin dresses, and opulent evening lamés from the twenties and thirties for movies and commercials. These dresses would be borrowed or bought outright by the models and worn in the evenings to black-tie parties and art-gallery openings. The press picked up this trend and reported it: In 1974 *The New York Times* did a story on special holiday-season dressing that featured my things. Some of these "dresses" were actually nightgowns or dressing gowns; but, because they were so beautifully detailed and styled, they easily passed for outerwear at night. Among my favorites are a wrap-waist, green silk-velvet dressing gown, cut on the bias, with trumpet sleeves. And a pale peach silk-chiffon peignoir with hand-scalloped edges, accordion tucking, and puffed sleeves, buttoning all the way down, which can be worn as a late-day dress as well as for evening (shown on pages 60–61).

In those early days, when I first opened my shop, there was an enormous selection of mint-condition vintage dresses available. One real find, a twenties rhinestone-studded black silk-chiffon dress, was bought by the Metropolitan Museum of Art for their costume collection shortly after I put it on the rack. Today, dresses like that are difficult to find (which accounts for their rising cost), but occasionally I turn up a gem.

One note on the dresses you'll be reading about here: During the years 1890 to 1950, dress manufacturers produced thousands of dresses. I'm not going to tell you about every style, every fabric. What I am going to do is to talk about those dresses that are standouts—the real fashion "finds" that are going to work for you—for day, for night, for an office. Today, the dresses to look for, the collectibles, are Edwardian "whites," beaded dresses (for evening), printed day dresses, anything velvet.

Above: *A good example of the kind of velvet or satin peignoir that can be worn at home or for evenings out.*

Right: *One of my favorite photographs of thirties dressing shows my mother (left front) shopping on the boardwalk in Atlantic City in 1933, wearing a midlength floral-printed chiffon dress with a cape (or "Bertha") collar.*

Far right: *This floral-printed, bias-cut, floor-length satin gown is one of the dresses in my collection of 1930s clothing most frequently rented for print and television ads.*

Left: *Barbara Greenwald's white Edwardian high-necked dress from her own collection is covered with eyelets and edged at hem and sleeve with layers of ruffles.*

Bottom: *Dyanne Silver's beautiful cotton Edwardian dress with handmade lace features the typical high neck and a soft lace ruffle at the yoke.*

Victorian and Edwardian Whites

After so many years of buying antique clothes from every era, I must say that I still succumb to a white dress. I swoon over white linen chemise-style dresses from the twenties. I love the simple drop-waist white afternoon dresses from 1918 to 1922. (Although you have to be careful: These dresses can look costume-y.) Show me a thirties dotted-swiss cotton day dress and I will burst into song. As far as I'm concerned, everyone should have at least one white dress in her closet—for day or evening. And if you can only afford to own one dress, it should be a white cotton lace dress from the Victorian or Edwardian period.

These turn-of-the-century floor-length dresses are made of lawn or batiste cotton in white or ecru, inset with eyelet lace or embroidered, and have high necks, tight sleeves, and occasionally "trains" (which can be removed). Each of these whites is handmade, one of a kind, from the rolled hem and covered buttons to the lace insets.

Not everyone can wear these dresses. Most of them, especially at the waistline, are very small. Edwardian dresses were made for petite women with tiny, corseted waists. So if you're small boned, you're in luck.

Edwardian whites make perfect wedding dresses and are a lot less expensive than new bridal gowns. Whites can also be worn for garden parties and warm-weather dressing, which makes them good "investment" clothing. If you think you might like to be married in an Edwardian dress, it's never too early to start looking, because these dresses are becoming more difficult to find. Some vintage-clothes shops specialize in white Victorian and Edwardian clothes. You can find at least one good shop that carries white in every major American city (see Part Three, Store Listings). Ask boutique owners to keep an eye out and to let you know when something comes in so that you can stop in and take a look at it. Many of my customers have bought Edwardian dresses to save for special occasions. In fact, I have kept one for years: an eyelet-embroidered, white linen dress, which I wore when I was married. For sentimental reasons, I could never sell it; so, on occasion, I lend it to a friend or rent it for commercials.

WHAT TO WEAR WITH WHITES

If your dress is made of sheer cotton batiste, it will require an underslip. The best choice is a brand-new, simple thin-strap slip, in white or beige, without too much detail or lace to detract from your dress.

The best accessories for whites are pearls or cameos. If you're going to wear a white dress as your wedding gown, wear pale bone stockings, with simple white satin pumps.

WHAT YOU SHOULD EXPECT TO PAY

Whites are expensive, especially in comparison with other vintage clothing. But they are worth the price if you consider that each is handmade and one of a kind. And for those women who have priced a new bridal gown, Edwardian dresses, in comparison, are bargains.

Whites in mint condition (i.e., suitable to wear as a wedding dress) cost hundreds of dollars. Depending on condition and the amount of restoration, they will probably cost between $500 and $1200; and in shops that specialize in Victorian and Edwardian things, they will cost more.

CARE

Most stores that carry whites sell them in immaculate condition—repaired, clean white, and starched. However, if you are lucky enough to find a "steal" rolled up in a ball at a flea market or hidden in your grandmother's attic, you can whiten it and try to rejuvenate it by following the bleaching instructions on pages 51–52.

Other tips to know before you purchase whites:

· Check stress areas on elbows and shoulder to see how worn the dress is and whether it needs repairing.
· Look for rust stains near metal hooks and eyes; these are sometimes impossible to remove.
· To remove wrinkles and creases: Do not steam your dress in the shower, as you would a tweed suit. Your dress fabric is too delicate. Instead, give it to the best dry cleaner you can find (ask friends to recommend one, or find a cleaner who specializes in wedding or ball gowns). Ask the cleaner to starch, press, and stuff it with tissue.

Twenties Beaded Evening Dresses

Beading—on dresses, shirts, jackets, shoe buckles—has been done for many years, but the best finds are the beaded evening gowns from the twenties, which are among the most exquisite dresses ever made. In the twenties the most sought-after beaded dresses were those designed in France by the Callot sisters, who ran the House of Callot, Paris. These dresses, famous for their intricate beaded patterning and couture quality, were snapped up by fashionable women in the States. Today, beaded Callot dresses are collectibles and can often be found at auctions.

Among the most beautiful beading you might be lucky enough to come across: crystal-clear or white glass beading, set on pale aqua or salmon-colored cotton batiste, for summer; iridescent or colorful rainbow (Venetian) beading on crepe de chine; black bugle, silver, or tiny caviar jet beading over black silk, for evening. For more color there is another version featuring black beading over red crepe. Also stunning at night: rhinestone-studded evening dresses sprinkled with tiny cut-glass slivers, usually on the front of the dress, at the hip, or sparkling along the hem—instant flash, without being flashy (*clinquant*, as the French say).

The beading is all hand sewn onto dress fabrics in patterns—florals or Deco geometrics—that decorate sleeves and necklines, border hems, or are inset in panels along each side, from shoulders to hem.

These dresses—in handwoven lawn, linen, or lightweight crepe de chine—were styled simply, along classic twenties lines: in either a basic chemise style, with no waist at all, or a simple tunic with a dropped waist that might be gathered, pleated, or flared at the hip; the neckline was usually a simple scoop; sleeveless, capped, or with long sleeves; and the hem always came to the knee or below.

The real treasures from this era are the all-over beaded dresses. Two from my collection are shown on page 65.

WHAT YOU SHOULD EXPECT TO PAY

You won't find any bargains if you're shopping for a beaded dress. In fact, consider yourself lucky if you find one in good condition at all. At auctions expect to pay between $200 and $400. If you find a beaded dress in fine condition at a vintage-clothes store, you will most likely pay a good deal more for it (between $300 and $800). The reason: Most of these dresses will have been restored, and cost for expensive restoration work will be passed on to the consumer.

CARE

Although I love beaded clothes, especially dresses, and am fascinated by their intricate patterning and handwork, I usually discourage people from owning them, because they are very difficult to care for. But if you want to own something beaded, here's some advice.

- When searching for anything beaded, try to buy it in nearly perfect condition. Check to see that the threads are strong and that the beads are not falling off. Some missing beads can be expected. Restoration is very expensive and difficult to do, and few people are willing to do it. Some of my customers have been successful in finding restorers for missing beadwork, holes, or fragile fabric; but most have found that they had to live without this kind of repair.
- If you want to try to find a restorer, contact a textile museum or an art museum in your town. Either one may be able to help you find someone specializing in this type of needlework near where you live. Bridal departments at local stores may be able to provide leads, too—since many new gowns have some beadwork.
- If beads loosen or fall off and you try replacing them yourself, back the area first with a piece of netting—it will help hold the beads in place.
- Never hang beaded clothes—especially completely beaded dresses, which are very heavy—on wire hangers. Wire hangers could accidentally cut into threading that holds the beading, and they also put stress on shoulder beadwork. Clothes that are trimmed with beading should be hung on padded hangers. All-over beaded dresses should be folded and kept in a drawer. If you want to wrap them, be sure they are covered in acid-free tissue paper.
- *Don't* dry-clean beaded clothing too frequently.
- *Don't* wash beaded clothing by hand—unless

Left: *Gina Davis wears a gem from my collection: white beads in a geometric motif on white silk—a straight chemise style, side slits, with hip gathers on either side, and elbow sleeve length.*

Bottom: *Peggy O'Dea wears one of her own favorites, a 1930s evening dress of blue net striped with iridescent blue sequins, with very high-heeled silver pumps.*

This red-and-pink floral print on black crepe is an elegant day or evening outfit. The neckline is black net with sequined appliqués in colors from the print.

you are experienced. Soap and water loosens beads; washing encourages thread breakage.

Printed Dresses of the Thirties, Forties, and Fifties

For vintage-clothes buyers and collectors, the really fun dresses to own are the full- or straight-skirt printed silk and rayon dresses made during the thirties, forties, and fifties. The first of these, all British-made, hit the vintage-clothes market in London in the late sixties; I went every two months to stock up. The English-made dresses, with their unexpected color combinations and intricate, abstract patterning, were, I think, among the most attractive day dresses ever designed. Five years later, American versions of printed day dresses appeared on the vintage-clothes circuit; and although they are versatile, beautiful additions to any working woman's wardrobe, the fabric design and the coloration of the English styles were, to me, bolder and more imaginative.

The styling of American-made printed day dresses was as varied as the printed silk or rayon fabrics they were made of. You'll find straight skirts with fitted tops; full skirts with blousy bodices; small collars and V-necks; and extra detailing, from shoulder pads and fishtails to peplums and bias godets (see Glossary)—depending on the decade in which the dresses were made. As a general rule thirties dresses were longer, with less-fitted waists; forties styling was more fitted at the waist and lengths were shorter; fifties dresses—"shirtwaist" styles—have longer lengths and fuller skirts.

Closings included zippers—under the arm or straight up the back—and as many as twenty buttons (covered or crystal on day versions, rhinestones for evening), running down the front from the neck to below the waist. Many of these dresses came with self-belts, made with matching fabric and molded-plastic (Celluloid) buckles. If a dress's belt is missing (usually it is), you can replace it by attaching ribbon or an elastic cinch to an original buckle—I (and I'm sure other dealers) have collected hundreds of buckles.

What's unique about these printed dresses is their coloration. You'll find everything from subdued "neutrals" (browns/beiges/bricks) and pastels (peach with lime, mauve with gray) to flashier, contrasting colors: printed mauve, chartreuse, and peach bordered in black; or bright reds and pale pinks on a cream-colored background. The most commonly used background colors for forties dresses were black, brown, and navy.

The patterning: everything from intricate, small designs—for example, baskets-of-flowers prints or dancing ballerinas of the forties to beautiful geometrics, often Art Deco inspired. Florals, including bold cabbage roses, plus the plaids and stripings done on silk taffetas, from the fifties.

Some printed day dresses have been "recycled" and the fabrics used to create new dresses. When these dresses first came on the market fifteen years ago, thousands of them, especially the larger sizes, were bought up by designers and boutique owners, who recut them into new designs by piecing new solid-color fabrics with the older prints to create dresses, skirts, and shirts. These are not vintage clothes, although they are made with vintage fabrics.

The "evening" version of the printed day dress comes from the early forties; it usually has a beaded or sequined neckline and tucked, three-quarter sleeves. One of the prettiest dresses in my collection is the bias-cut, soft-gathered crepe, with a hydrangea-printed fabric in shades of blues and pinks against black, and a sequins-over-black-netting silhouette neckline shown on page 66.

Also made in the forties were the wonderful all-black versions of these dresses, in rayon or silk, often beaded or sequined, with padded shoulders, peplums, or fishtail detailing. These increasingly popular little black dresses look best worn a bit shorter, with textured stockings. A general rule: Keep them just below the knee, rather than mid-calf as most women have been wearing dresses.

HOW TO WEAR A PRINTED DRESS

Most of these printed dresses will take you through the day from morning through night, depending on how you accessorize, how you dress them "up" or "down."

- If you're wearing a rayon chiffon, you can make it work for day by putting a cardigan sweater over it; if there's a collar, wear it out as

This bias-cut, floor-length, printed silk-chiffon thirties evening dress of mauve, gray, yellow, and lilac looks captivating on Amanda Stinchecum for a special "at home" party.

shown on page 100. Or you could dress it down with a blazer (in wool or linen, depending on the season).

· Bold cabbage-rose patterns or very colorful designs can be "muted" by slipping a solid-color cashmere sweater (slipover) over your dress (again, with the collar worn out).

· Colorful lizard or leather belts look great wrapped at the waists of the fuller forties day dresses. Pick belts that match the background color. Or pick up a color from the printed pattern (often pink, red, lavender, or beige).

· Another way of wearing a printed day dress: with a leotard and tights in the same color underneath and flat ballet slippers, all matching one of the colors of the print.

· A dressier look for cocktails or dinner: Wear black net stockings and open-toed pumps with a black-print dress.

· With a multicolor purple/red/cream flower-printed dress, writer Alexandra Penney wears cowboy boots and an off-white crew-neck sweater in winter; she goes barer—with just a beige slip underneath—in warmer weather months, making hers a seasonless dress.

WHAT YOU SHOULD EXPECT TO PAY

By today's standards printed dresses are bargains. Stores that collect them in quantity offer the best pricing. As a guideline: Expect to pay between $50 and $60 for an average-looking printed day dress in good condition. A more interesting dress from this period, beaded or sequined, in the best condition, may range from $50 to $100. The more exceptional dresses—evening versions, those made of pure silk, with very special detailing—will cost over $100.

CARE

Customers often ask me if they can wash these rayon and silk printed dresses, but I advise against it. Although I have heard some hand-washing success stories—cleaned in Woolite and cold water, air-dried on a plastic hanger, and then pressed with a warm iron—I think you are taking a chance. Hand-washed rayon crepes may shrink (by as many as three sizes), and the dyes, which are often not colorfast, may run. Bias-cut fabrics may stretch if ironed improperly; and some fabrics retain a sheen if pressed with a too-hot iron. To be safe, have printed dresses dry-cleaned.

Some of these dresses can still be found in never-worn condition. If you come across one that's not new, check its condition by looking at the underarms and the general fabric strength before buying it.

Often hems will need to be let down. Check for fading at the fold line and on the underside of the hem. Dry cleaning and steaming old creases will usually remove traces of their old life if there is no fading.

A peach, turquoise, red, and white floral print on navy crepe worn with turquoise snakeskin shoes. The lace shoulder insets add a special detail often found on English printed day dresses.

Velvets

Ten years ago, panne-, silk-, or rayon-velvet dresses from the twenties through the fifties were at their height of popularity. Now they're making a comeback, especially among Europeans. A vintage-clothes dealer visiting from France told me that French women who wear vintage things want velvets for day, but that she can't find enough here to take home.

Next to beading and sequins, velvet makes the most elegant-looking dresses around, especially the body-skimming Garbo-esque velvet evening gowns from the twenties and thirties, with low scoop backs, cowl necks, and long sleeves slit at the shoulder. Most of these twenties and thirties dresses of panne and flocked velvets were really dressing gowns, waist wrapped, kimono sleeved, with long, sweeping bias-cut skirts, designed to be worn at home in the evening. One of these in my collection is the trumpet-sleeved, sea-green velvet gown shown on pages 60–61.

The coloring of the velvet fabrics is another detail that sets these dresses apart from any others. Twenties silk velvets were dyed in beautiful shades ranging from dark—jet blacks and rich chocolate browns—to wonderful pale sherbet color—lime, pink, cream, salmon. In the thirties, deeper colors—hunter green, purple, burgundy, fuchsia, aqua—were added. Then, in the forties and fifties, silks were replaced by rayon and cotton velvets. Colors became a bit brighter, less subtle—rust, navy blue in the forties; reds and greens in the fifties—because of the way these fabrics picked up the dyes.

Other styles to look for include the fitted-to-the-waist, flared little "princess" dresses of the forties and the full-skirted Anne Fogarty dresses popular in the fifties.

WHAT YOU SHOULD EXPECT TO PAY

Condition, detailing, styling, and color all play a part in determining the cost of velvets. The elegant twenties and thirties dresses, made of beautiful colored silk velvet, with beading or sequins (and sometimes chiffon flowers, added to the waist) will cost over $100, as will elaborately flocked designs. A little less expensive are rayon-velvet and cotton-velveteen day dresses from the fifties, which average about $50 or $60.

CARE

- Velvets, when they're old, "give" around the shoulders and the underarms. Always check the condition of these stress points, because it is difficult to repair velvet (other than along the seams).
- Be sure the velvet feels soft, supple to the touch; old silk velvet is very fragile.
- The dresses of the twenties were made with long, tight sleeves. Be sure you can move your arms comfortably, without ripping sleeves.
- *Never* hand wash or press velvet. Always have it dry-cleaned.
- Velvet is a very delicate fabric. If you get it wet—spill something on it or get caught in the rain—it could spot or the nap can be flattened; have the dress cleaned as soon as possible.

Rita Hayworth in beaded 1940s white crepe two-piece dress with shoulder pads, slit front, and platform shoes—the epitome of forties glamour.

9

Blouses: Instant Look-Turners

You can pair them with skirts or pants, changing the look of either to dress up or dress down an outfit: Blouses are instant look-turners. Writer Alexandra Penney has the right idea. She collects handmade silk blouses from the thirties and forties, especially those with yokes, embroidered collars, and small pin tucking—an endless variety of colors and styles that can "circulate" through her wardrobe, sometimes teamed with black velvet skirt, sometimes tucked into pants or worn under a knitted sweater, always with pins or pearls. Here are the blouses to look for, to buy.

Victorian/Edwardian Shirtwaists

Anyone who knows anything about vintage clothing knows about the handmade Victorian and Edwardian whites coveted by dealers and customers. You have undoubtedly seen a typical white with its basic silhouette of high neck, lace cuffs, buttoning all the way down the front or back with covered or hand-crocheted buttons. If you haven't seen an authentic vintage "white" blouse, you most certainly have seen a copy; because as the demand for these vintage blouses has increased— and the supply dwindled—manufacturers have stepped up their reproductions of the style.

As a lover of whites, I had some of the first and most beautiful handmade Victorian blouses ever seen in New York City when I was in my Thirteenth Street shop in 1966. They attracted a growing clientele, among them Julie Christie, who was a regular customer, and the photographer Maureen Lambray, who collected whites. The handmade Victorian whites are treasures, truly unmistakable with their leg-o'-mutton sleeves (more about these later)—in white or ecru cotton, linen, batiste, or lawn—edged or inset with handmade imported lace, or hand embroidered. They're luxurious, flattering to everyone with their flash of white at the throat that accentuates a long neck, or makes a short neck look better.

Wearing a white blouse makes you feel very feminine. If you are lucky enough to find one of these blouses with French, Belgian, or Alençon lace set into the sleeves, edging the bodice and the high-neck collar, you have one of the most sensuous pieces of clothing ever made—not to mention its versatility, its ability to "turn" almost everything in your wardrobe. For instance, with a tuxedo for evening it is a "softener," an unusual contrast. With a white petticoat, it can be a wedding or afternoon dress. Or mixed with a sweater or tweed suit, it becomes classic dinner dressing. There are, by the way, some Victorian/Edwardian black blouses with the same delicate styling of the whites (one is shown in the photograph at the opening of the chapter), but whites remain the more desirable of the two.

A few words about the fit of a Victorian blouse. It's characterized by a high neck, long sleeves—either slightly puffed or leg-o'-mutton-styled—and tails of different lengths, the front ones always much longer than those in back. Many people think *leg-o'-mutton* means a sleeve that is puffed at the shoulder. Not true. If you imagine what a leg of lamb looks like, the sleeve shape is clear: It is puffed at the top, gradually becoming more slender and then fitting close at the wrist. Usually the puff extends to the elbow; the lower sleeve is more tightly fitted from elbow to wrist. The reason the front tails are long and the back ones are short is that for many years women stood in the "kangaroo stoop"—with their bosoms thrust forward and their derrieres out in back. At the back of each blouse was a piece of tape ending in a string tie sewn on at the waist, with two optional eye hooks. The string tie wrapped the waist and held the front of the blouse down, while the back eye hook, which attached to the skirt waistband, kept the blouse from coming out in back. Pretty complicated! Today, most women either live with the back tails shorter than the front ones, shorten the front tails to match the back, or add fabric to the back, making it even with the front.

The most important thing about buying whites is to examine the strength of the cotton, lace, or linen fabric. Fine cotton-batiste blouses should be handled with great care and be worn infrequently

Above: *An embroidered linen collarless Edwardian blouse, which designer Linda Rodin wears with front tails out over linen pants of her own design.*

Right: *Gina Davis is ready for her afternoon wedding in an Edwardian blouse over an eyelet-embroidered linen petticoat, belted with a scarf tie to give the effect of a peplum. Inset shows a close-up of the high-necked Edwardian blouse of handkerchief linen with ruffled jabot front, tucked lace cuffs, and covered back buttons.*

(if you want them to last!). Sturdier muslins and heavyweight linens can stand more wear and tear. Remember: You are buying a garment that is eighty years old—or older. Because most Victorian blouses were handmade or custom-made, there are no size markings. Also, waists will be higher and shoulders narrower than on a new blouse. Try on any blouse before buying it; and check necks,

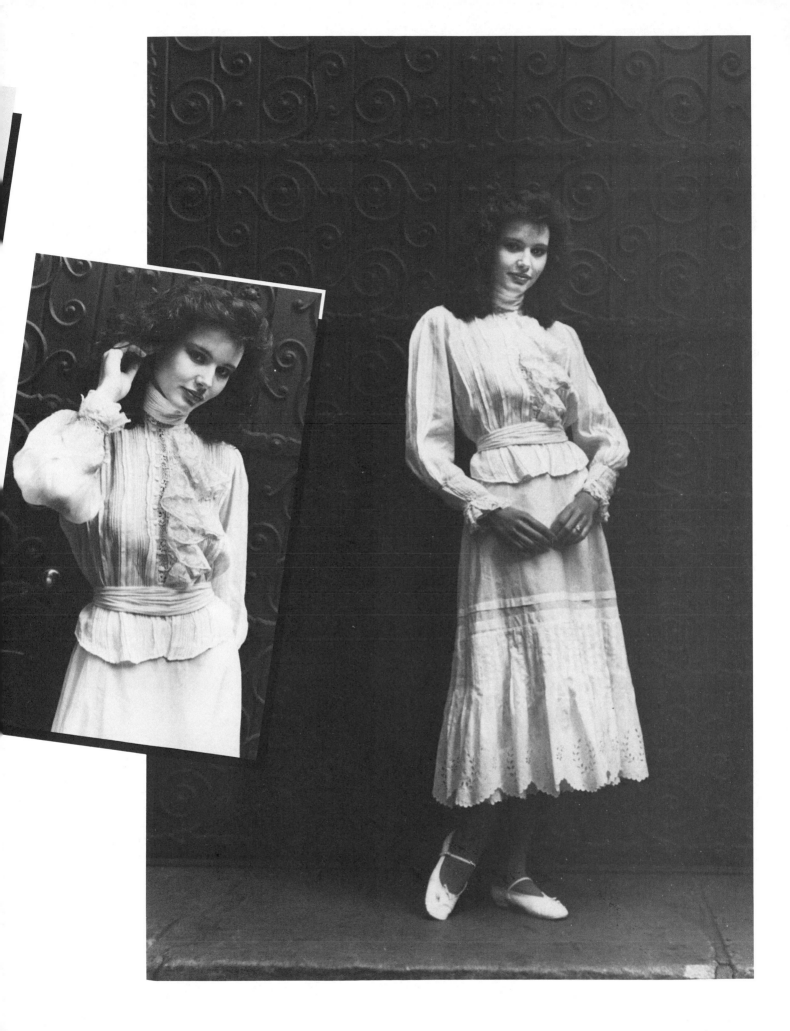

underarms, and elbows for repairs and weak fibers. Even a blouse in perfect condition may not last through careless wearings, disco dances, or general wear-and-tear abuse.

WHAT YOU SHOULD EXPECT TO PAY

When looking for a mint-condition, handmade, lace-inset Victorian/Edwardian blouse, keep in mind that you are buying a very special item—these are not cheap anymore. The highest prices will be at stores specializing in whites; vintage-clothes shops that carry just a few whites will be slightly less expensive.

A very ordinary-looking blouse, made of muslin, with some detail and in less-than-perfect condition, runs about $75 to $125. Those in excellent condition may go as high as $200 or $300 for a blouse that is exceptional. It is not unusual for these blouses to cost even more, especially those made of silk or handkerchief linen, with handmade lace insets. These could cost anywhere from $400 to $500 and up.

HOW TO WEAR WHITE SHIRTWAISTS

My three favorite ways to wear a classic lace or embroidered white Victorian blouse:

· With straight-leg linen pants, the front tails outside the pants and the shorter back ones left short, as worn by Linda Rodin (see illustration).
· As a spring/summer bridal outfit tucked into a gathered white cotton petticoat trimmed with crocheting or lace and tied with sherbet-colored taffeta ribbon or an embroidered silk fabric belt at the waist (see illustration).
· As a suit blouse, tucked into a tweed or linen shirt.
· Other ways of wearing whites: with linen shorts . . . with black velvet anything . . . accessorized with pearls or with a small enamel pin.

Twenties Blouses: Deco . . . Beaded

Before women started buying antique clothes in vintage boutiques, they knew about flapper clothing and could always put their hands on a beaded twenties dress for a costume party. The twenties

era produced some of the most beautiful clothing ever designed for women. Besides designing the classic suit that carries her name, Coco Chanel also designed the chemise-style dress. And Fortuny, the Italian designer of fabrics, furnishings, and fashion, is best known for his pleated tea dresses of the twenties, which have been the major source of inspiration today for the designer Mary McFadden. The detail, the styling, the sweep of the fabrics of twenties clothing are still being copied today.

To find a twenties beaded silk evening blouse, or one made of crepe and lamé, or a simple suit blouse of cotton and lace with Celluloid buttons is a treat. The shape, of course, is totally different from a Victorian or an Edwardian blouse; the waist is dropped, the neck lower, the sleeve and cuff looser. The looser styling and the raglan sleeve of these blouses make them easier for most women to wear. But don't be fooled by appearances: The blouse may look bigger on the hanger than it really is—this is the style. Once you have tried it on, you will see that the size is not as large as it appears.

The twenties is an era of both exquisite simplicity and all-out decoration. One of the best things about twenties blouses is their variety—silks, satins, crepes, chiffons; often with beads or embroidery. You can find a basic navy cotton blouson with a square sailor collar for day as easily as a knockout crepe de chine covered in Venetian beading in an Art Deco style. Beaded blouses, like beaded dresses, may present an upkeep problem, because the weight of the beading can tear the fabric or the beads can come loose. For how to care for beading, see pages 64–65.

Twenties bright-colored cotton blouses for day, with soft square necklines and lace trimming are another prize. The best have tucking and hem stitching around the cuffs or collar. (One note: There were no fitted bustlines at this time; so be prepared for a loose torso with an accent on the hipline.) The coloring of twenties fabric dyes is mouth-watering: everything from cottons and silks in pale sherbet tones and shades of blue, cream, and mint, to deeper greens, rusts, grays, and burgundy. Prints, too, are rich in variety: solids, printed abstract Art Deco designs, geometrics, or—the rarest—printed jacquard weaves. Metallic

Left: *Linda Rodin's linen shorts add a contemporary feeling to this loosely cut, low-waisted 1920s blouse of cream-colored silk. Notice the lace-trimmed neck, hem, and inset. Below: Turquoise crepe de chine 1920s blouse with iridescent blue beading at the neck, around the sleeve edge, and at the scalloped hem. The raglan sleeve and loose style make it an easy blouse to wear over soft silk pants.*

threads, copper, gold, and silver, were woven into some fabrics, too.

In my private collection is a twenties blouse of exceptional quality: turquoise crepe de chine with iridescent blue beading in an American Indian geometric pattern on the front. I wear it frequently with simple black linen pants (in warmer weather, I switch to shorts) to avoid a costume-y look.

WHAT YOU SHOULD EXPECT TO PAY

For a simple cotton twenties blouse with lace trim or Celluloid buttons, expect to pay about $50. Collectible beaded blouses are harder to find, and you won't come across many. When you do, they could run $100 if they are in good condition. In mint condition, twenties evening blouses—either beaded, embroidered, or pin tucked—could cost $150 or more.

The Thirties: New Shape, New Style

The ensemble—dress, coat, with matching hat and gloves—became so important in the thirties that the blouse, as an individual item, took a back seat. Sometimes blouses were part of the ensemble, worn over a "skirt" attached to a slip top. But although they are scarce, thirties blouses are available, with one difference in styling: The twenties accentuated the hip and derriere with bows and sashes; the thirties focused more on the waist by pushing it up—almost to where it belonged. The bustline was more shaped, too; sleeves were set-in rather than raglan, with a puffed or gathered shoulder and lapel collars. Or they were asymmetric with wide-swooping collars, buttoning on the side. Satins, silks, cottons, and some rayons—frequently bias cut—were the fabrics used for thirties blouses, and they were often finished with special details, such as self-belts or mother-of-pearl buttons. The prettiest, most wearable thirties blouses were made of chiffon with pin tucks, lace detail, and pearl buttons, an example of which is on page 77. I had a similar blouse on display once, and when the photographer Maureen Lambray called up to ask if anything super special had come into the shop recently, I thought of this lovely, intricate piece of workmanship. She ended

up buying it and giving it to Jeanne Moreau for a wedding present.

Evening blouses of the thirties were made of ivory or cream silk crepe or silk chiffon and had exquisite detailing—sometimes satin cuffs finished with hand-sewn buttonholes and crystal buttons, handmade lace collars or yokes, tiny pin tucking, or appliquéd satin insets. Other detailing included hem stitching, embroidery, and hand-carved mother-of-pearl buttons.

WHAT YOU SHOULD EXPECT TO PAY

You can still find a very simple thirties shirt blouse in a flea market for $15 to $45. This is where the *Village Voice*'s style editor, Mary Peacock, collects hers, usually pairing them with a simple gray skirt, which has become her working "uniform." The pure silk, satin, or chiffon versions, with pin tucks, lace collars and cuffs, or fine buttons, start at $85 and can run as high as $150. Rayon versions and those handmade in France cost about $60.

Forties and Fifties Blouses: Availability Plus

Most of the vintage blouses found today date from the late forties and fifties. Clothing was scarcer during the war, Europeans were not manufacturing much clothing, and Americans were using most of their fabric for uniforms and the war effort. To replace silk, which was being used for parachutes, rayon and rayon acetate began to

---

Left: *A simple white rayon blouse from the 1940s—short sleeved, openwork detail on back shoulder, and pearl buttons—tucked into slightly pegged black pants, which have a self-belt. Black and white: a clean, workable look.*

Top right: *A super-soft chiffon blouse with the works: lace-trimmed cuffs and collar, tucks galore, oval-shaped lace insets, pearl buttons, worn with a 1920s paste bar pin at the neck.*

Bottom right: *This dressy silk-chiffon blouse with its lace jabot, ruffled cuffs, and lightly padded shoulder can go a long way in Phyllis Posnick's wardrobe. Here worn with linen bermuda shorts, it can also work wonders for a simple suit.*

The kind of folk blouse to look for: a cross-stitched, hand-embroidered chiffon Rumanian blouse—blue on cream—made in the 1930s.

be used on a large scale. During the war years, a simple rayon blouse with a patch pocket and a sporty uniform style was the look of the day. These were produced in every color, and there was little or no handwork on them. Recycled today, they are still wearable and easy to care for, and they work perfectly with suits, sweaters, or a pair of jeans.

The padded-shoulder look (always in and out of style) became popular in the late thirties and continued into the forties. Sometimes the "pad" was a piece of buckram sewn into the shoulder seam to make the sleeve puff out, imitating the Edwardian sleeve style. More often, the pad exaggerated the shoulders, making them look higher and wider. By broadening the shoulders, the waistline seemed smaller and the hips slimmer.

One of the most collectible forties styles has padded cap sleeves, a jewel neck, and covered buttons down the back. It can be decorated with everything from beading or sequins to buttons, bows, and pin tucking, to hand-painted pictures— sometimes of poodles—down the front. (You can see one version of this blouse—a short-sleeved black silk, with a beaded jewel neckline—on page 107.) These blouses work perfectly under suits because the focus is on the front. One way to wear a blouse like this is the way California designer Bonnie Strauss does, which I love: backwards, as a jacket with a simple camisole underneath, so the beading or detailing shows off in back. These particular blouses are usually made of rayon crepe, in every color from rust and gray to magenta and pink.

The romantically named Morlove Company made another typical forties style in many basic colors such as peach, white, or black rayon crepe for day, with long sleeves, a tight wrist cuff, buttons down the front, and a yoke of machine-made lace.

WHAT YOU SHOULD EXPECT TO PAY

For a very simple, very plain forties blouse with pin tucking or a small collar and padded shoulders, expect to pay about $50. Evening blouses, those with sequins, beading, or hand painting, in rayon or silk begin at $100. Silk shirtwaist styles from the fifties with roll-up sleeves, front buttons, and Peter Pan collars (most frequently made by the MacMullen Company) run about $40. Nylon blouses with fake tucking or rhinestones cost less, about $15 to $30.

Folksy, Ethnic Blouses

A popular style of many vintage-clothes collectors is the Hungarian or Rumanian "peasant" blouse made of chiffon, silk crepe, or cotton and embroidered with a simple cross-stitch or a multicolored floral or geometric pattern. There is a folksy feeling to most of these blouses, which were very popular with vintage-clothes buyers in the late sixties and early seventies and are becoming stylish again. The best are made of multicolor embroidered silk chiffon and are sought by buyers who love handmade things. Another favorite: the short-sleeved cotton version with multicolor embroidery.

WHAT YOU SHOULD EXPECT TO PAY

For an embroidered all-cotton folk blouse, with long or short sleeves, made in Hungary or Rumania, expect to pay $75 or more. The silk-chiffon versions of these, embroidered with cross-stitching, cost about $100 to $150.

Care

The best advice I give my customers about caring for their blouses is to stop washing and ironing any blouse that is not made of cotton—especially those made of silk and rayon crepe. Careless hot-water washings can shrink them to child size. Their detailing is too complicated, too, for someone unskilled with an iron. Be sure to examine carefully and in a good light any blouse that you're planning to buy, look for worn areas, especially around the shoulders, under the arms, and along buttonhole edges. Don't buy blouses that have yellowed perspiration stains under the arms, because most dry cleaners cannot remove them.

For care of a Victorian/Edwardian white, see washing instructions on pages 51–52. If you prefer to have your blouse dry-cleaned, have it sized, too—a dry-cleaning process that adds a little stiffening.

Care should be taken with all twenties clothing, especially blouses, because they are irreplaceable. Avoid what I call the "early drip-dry look"—blouses with faded fabrics or colors that have run into each other—neither of these can be restored. Repeatedly washing a silk or cotton blouse that has run will not improve it.

Also on the subject of hand washing: Unless a folk blouse has a "colorfast" label, do not hand wash it either; have it dry-cleaned.

If you own a forties blouse in net or chiffon with a hand-painted picture, treat it carefully! Have it dry-cleaned only; and tell your cleaner that the design is hand painted.

The rebeading of a blouse that is missing whole areas of beads is considered "restoration." Few professionals are capable of doing this type of work—or want to—as it is very time-consuming. It is also expensive. For more on beading and its care, see pages 64–65.

10

Shirts: Versatility Plus

Today, more rack space in vintage-clothes stores is devoted to men's shirts than to almost any other single category. Availability is one reason. Popularity is another: Men's shirting from the 1900s through the 1950s is bought not only by men but by women who have realized how wearable—and versatile—a man's oversized shirt can be. The shirts to own, to collect—by the dozens, as many of my customers do—are "gab" shirts, cowboy shirts, Hawaiian shirts, collarband shirts.

"Gab" Shirts

"Gab" shirts are named for the fabric they're made of: gabardine, a diagonal-line twill pattern woven into fabrics of wool, cotton, or rayon. Gabardine shirts are classic men's shirting: almost always full cut, with long sleeves, a pointed collar, and two breast-patch pockets (with or without buttons or flaps). Gab shirts from the early fifties were manufactured in a beautiful and unusual rainbow of colors, which is one of the things that makes them so appealing. They range from pale sherbets—bananas, pinks, lemons—to bright brights—magenta, chartreuse. The hardest-to-find colorings are bright red, black, chartreuse, and apricot. If you find one of these, hold on to it!

In the later fifties, more detailing was added to men's gab shirts: contrasting trim and piping, initial and emblem embroidery, and edge-stitching. Harder to find, but worth looking for: gab shirts with contrasting yokes and inverted back pleats.

I've been selling gab shirts for ten years, and customers always want to know where my "new" ones are. What makes gabs so popular, besides their colorings, is that, like jeans, they're basic, inexpensive, and made to last. And, like jeans, they look good on everyone. Gab shirts are classic, simple men's shirting: well made, of good, soft, lasting fabrics.

HOW TO WEAR GABS

The simplest, most casual way for women to wear men's gab shirts is belted over jeans, with rolled sleeves. A small or medium size is the best choice for most women, although the shoulders may drop slightly and the sleeves may be a little too long. Rolling the sleeves gives the shirt an easier, more casual look and saves on repair or alteration of the cuffs. It is easy to shorten the sleeves by removing the cuff, cutting the sleeve to the wrist, and then reattaching the cuff.

Men wear gab shirts tucked into pleated pants, khakis, or jeans; cowboy or beaded Italian belts give the look a Western turn.

Many women find the small-size gabs work well with suits, with a marcasite pin at the neck and a collection of paste bracelets. Another version: buttoning the shirt to the neck and wearing it with a bowtie; the most fun ones are brightly polka-dotted.

Another way to wear a gab shirt is as a jacket, over a blouse or a V-neck T-shirt in a contrasting color.

However you wear a man's gab shirt, be sure it is loose and slightly bloused.

WHERE TO FIND, WHAT TO PAY

Gab shirts (as well as the other shirts you'll be reading about here) can be found in varying condition in almost every vintage-clothes shop. In big cities, such as Los Angeles and New York, they are sold in flea markets, too. The price range is wide, depending on condition and uniqueness.

During the late sixties, men's shirts from 1900 to the fifties cost a few dollars. Now the prices, especially for the most unusual ones, have gone up, primarily because these shirts are harder to find. For a gab shirt in good condition, with trim, flap, or patch pockets, in an unusual color, expect to pay about $35 and up. One exception: extra-large sizes, because they are in less demand, are usually less expensive.

Cowboy Shirts

The most sought-after collectibles are cowboy and Hawaiian shirts. The best of these walk out of my store the same day I put them on the rack. Not long ago I put an extraordinary cowboy shirt—rhinestone-studded, with multicolored appliquéd peacocks on black gabardine—in my window. The next morning I found a blank check under my door, with a note that said, "I don't care what it costs, I want that shirt!" He paid the ticket price—$95 (1979 price).

The craze for anything cowboy started long before today's fashion designers "discovered" the Western trend. Since 1970 elaborately designed cowboy shirts have been among the hottest vintage items, snapped up by collectors despite their rising cost (which is still about half the price of a new one).

The best cowboy shirts are made of rayon gabardine and come from the forties and fifties (although cotton cowboy shirts from the sixties are much easier to find). The basic, standard-looking cowboy shirt (and therefore the least expensive) is the solid-color cowboy with contrasting piping around the collar, cuffs, yoke, and slash pockets, in color combinations such as brown with cream, or dark blue against light blue. The real finds, however, are the more elaborate rodeo shirts, worn by cowboys for dressing up or for competitions. A favorite of mine is an unusual black-and-gold-lurex rayon-faille forties cowboy shirt, with padded shoulders and pearl buttons—simple, wearable, great color combination.

The most collectible cowboys, from the fifties, were machine-embroidered by the H Bar C Company (a label to shop for, along with Rock Mount Ranch Wear). Other rodeo shirts were basic cowboy shirts that were hand embroidered and appliquéd by girl friends and wives.

Among the most unusual cowboys to look for: embroidered yokes in contrasting colors, with cord piping, and (optional) satin or leather fringe. The yoke embroidery (either hand- or machine-

---

Top left: *A timeless 1950s rayon-gab shirt in tan with bottle-green collar and sleeves; two breast pockets with buttoned flaps.*

Top right: *Details on cowboy shirt: dark burgundy yoke, with appliquéd hearts and machine embroidery, and double-stitched pocket, piped in tan.*

Bottom: *A light blue rayon-gabardine cowboy shirt with a dark blue yoke embroidered in blue, red, and yellow, with pearl snaps on front and cuffs.*

done) determines the shirt's value. The most sought-after cowboy shirts are those embroidered with themes; Western landscapes—with cactus and desert flowers; animal scenes of cows, horses, steers; a cowpoke's basics, including boots, lassos; or "gambling themes," embroidered with hearts, diamonds, clubs, spades, and playing cards. Another detail to look for: mother-of-pearl snaps up the front and on the cuffs.

HOW TO WEAR COWBOYS

Cowboy shirts appeal to everyone—to men, women, and even bankers, lawyers, and business execs. People love wearing cowboy shirts, for the fun of it, for the whimsical alternative they offer to an everyday suit-and-tie uniform.

Many men wear cowboys with a sports jacket and jeans. The accessory that brings the whole look together: a good leather belt with a western buckle. Some men go completely cowboy, wearing etched-silver collar tips and string ties with steer-head slides.

Women wear cowboy shirts under suits (with or without a string tie) for a casual look. It should be worn as you would a man's gab shirt: belted over jeans, as a jacket, and so forth.

If you see a great cowboy shirt, don't pass it up because you can't think of anything to wear with it. A cowboy shirt works with more things in your wardrobe than you'd imagine—*if* you don't think of it strictly as cowboy gear. If the shirt is black, white, or gray, for instance, you can team it with a pair of black wool pants. A brown or green cowboy looks great under a Harris tweed jacket.

If you're lucky enough to find an old Arizona-style fringed suede jacket, put it over your shirt and wear it with jeans or khakis.

A good cowboy shirt is a collector's item. You can always hang it on the wall!

WHERE TO FIND, WHAT TO PAY

Today, serious collectors really have to hunt to find the most magnificent-looking rodeo shirts. If you're shopping for one, check out vintage-clothes stores first and then other sources in your area, such as flea markets. The best cowboy shirts are usually found in New York, Los Angeles, and San Francisco, although there is also a good supply in Denver.

Some antique-clothing stores stock all the vintage cowboy shirts they can find, regardless of condition. Check for underarm stains (cowboys sweat a lot), frayed cuffs and collars, and missing or broken snaps (these can easily be replaced).

The easier-to-find cotton cowboy shirts of the sixties (these are more fitted) and simple fifties rayon-gab cowboys cost about $50. Well-made, machine-embroidered cowboy shirts in good condition go for over $100 today. And elaborately hand-embroidered rodeos are even more.

Hawaiian Shirts

Hawaiian shirts—short-sleeved sports shirts for men, with colorful, splashy prints (made in both Hawaii and the States)—became popular during the forties postwar period. Some Hawaiians were brought back by military men stationed in the Pacific. Others were brought back by people traveling to the Hawaiian Islands on vacation. Hawaiian shirts, with their abstract "pictorials" of Hawaiian paradise and their "welcome to Hawaii" slogans, were part of the tourist paraphernalia hawked to vacationers as travel mementos and were sold in souvenir shops and hotel lobbies.

Hawaiian shirts became even more popular in the United States when, in 1953, Montgomery Clift appeared wearing one in *From Here to Eternity*. American companies jumped on the Hawaiian-shirt bandwagon, manufacturing flower-printed versions for men's leisure and warm-weather wear. Although most Hawaiians are open-necked, short-sleeved sports shirts, occasionally you may come across a long-sleeved version.

The early Hawaiian shirts (from the forties and fifties, shorter in length than a regular man's shirt and made of silk or rayon) are works of art; they're now highly collectible, expensive, and difficult to find. One of my treasures from the forties, made in Hawaii by Kuu-Ipo, is chartreuse, orange, and white on dark blue, picturing Hawaiian men surfing, three bare-breasted Hawaiian women dancing, and a man playing a guitar under a palm tree. Ribboning the scene are the words *Waikiki, Hawaii, Molokai,* and *Aloha.* On the back it says *State of Hawaii,* with *Honolulu* and *Hawaii* printed underneath. The buttons (the ones to look for) are carved coconut. Another star

I have is a red rayon shirt made in Hawaii by Pikaki. An abstract figurative, it depicts yellow-bordered black figures throwing javelins at bright yellow fish. In the distance, you can see the isles of Hawaii, surrounded by flower leis and black pineapples against a white ground.

Besides primitives, there are other Hawaiian shirt categories—pineapples, florals, Japanese motifs. These, too, appeal to collectors. Carl Wilson of the Beach Boys is a Hawaiian-shirt collector; he reportedly owns eighty or a hundred. The song-writer and performer Peter Allen has collected about fifty shirts. Among his favorites: a Navajo sand painting and a heavyweight rayon Hawaiian, American-made by the McGregor Company, with a Japanese country scene.

Original Hawaiian shirts of rayon challis, with primitives depicting Hawaiian people in native dress, are also highly prized; as is any shirt signed by a designer. And shirts with a label from Duke Kahanamoku, an Olympics gold-medalist who lent his name to a line of Hawaiians, have a special cachet for collectors. One of his classics is the rare and sought-after two-color pineapple print—white pineapples against a solid dark background (pineapple shirts have been copied widely).

Still harder to find are Hawaiian-style silk shirts with Japanese motifs: pine trees, egrets, helmets, arrows, and Samurai.

Many American companies (including Penney's, Cisco, Art Vogue, Duke of Hollywood) made beautiful Hawaiians in the fifties. A typical American-made "pleasure shirt," made by a company called Mark Twain, shows an abstract scenario of black-and-white huts under yellow palm trees against a red ground. Another, made in California by Random Wear and labeled "authentically styled," has a pale-rust background against which melon-covered bodies race across the fabric carrying nets, with a border of black-and-yellow pineapples, green palm trees, and florals. The words *Halekulani Hotel, Molokai* are scribbled in white. The best American-made shirts have mother-of-pearl buttons and patch pockets that match up perfectly to the shirt's print.

Florals are another category of Hawaiians. Some were made in Hawaii; others, known as California florals, were made in the States. Among the favorites in my collection is a gray-and-white, flower-

Pink Hawaiian women with black hair and green grass skirts are prominent on this pale chartreuse rayon shirt from the early fifties, worn with dark green gab pants.

Left: *Robert Kitchen poses in front of one of his well-known Hawaiian shirt paintings, wearing the tropical fish shirt that served as a model.* Below: *One of Eliot Hubbard's flashier, bolder, floral-print rayon fifties Hawaiians. This one has a red background with a white, blue, and yellow print.* Opposite: *Gina's and Norman's colorful printed shirts always look good worn with jeans and a beaded Indian or tooled cowboy belt.*

and-leaves print on red rayon, covered with starfish. Hawaiian-made orchid prints are more difficult to find, and anything printed in yellow, green, white, or pink, especially on a black background, is very rare and sought after for its color alone.

Eliot Hubbard, Director of Publicity at CBS Records, has been collecting Hawaiians, mostly florals, since 1974. "I never thought of them as collectible, until I came upon a beautiful old shirt—a white-on-red floral—and I've been hooked ever since." Eliot has about six favorites—all forties flower prints in soft, subtle colors—which he wears over and over again, "with painter's pants or jeans in the office, where I dress casually; under suits when I have to go to corporate events." He adds other flashier, bolder floral prints to his collection (which now numbers ninety and is valued in the thousands of dollars) at the rate of one every five or six weeks, but never wears them.

Among the shirts in Eliot's collection: a salmon-on-mustard border-print floral (popular in the forties); a red-and-white-on-mustard flower print with chartreuse leaves; a pale pink-and-green bamboo print on burgundy (a hard-to-find background color). Eliot's favorites are a multicolor-on-green printed "Matson Line" figurative, designed by Eugene Savage and sold (or given) to first-class passengers aboard the Matson Line's California-to-Hawaii cruises. And a Gauguin-style Royal Hawaiian Hotel primitive of red-yellow-green on black rayon, splashed with jumping fish, and made in Hawaii by Aloha, for which Eliot paid $130.

HOW TO WEAR HAWAIIANS

Hawaiian shirts are versatile and can be worn summer and winter, by men and women.

- Pair them with jeans, with white cotton shorts, or with anything linen in summer.
- Wear them all winter under a solid-color Shetland pullover, with the collar out.
- To contrast styles, to soften a conservative look, Asher Jason sometimes wears his red-blue-yellow-white palm tree and flower Hawaiian under his navy Cerutti suit, with a blue knitted tie and, for the fun of it, a yellow and blue printed

Roy Rogers cowboy handkerchief tucked in the jacket pocket.

· Wear a Hawaiian open to the waist over a pretty camisole with a simple white Edwardian petticoat.

· Try a fitted white-piqué vest over your shirt; wear it with navy or white pants or Bermuda shorts.

· Accessorize Hawaiian shirts inexpensively with thirties plastic Deco jewelry. Examples: a red carved bangle bracelet . . . a dangly fruit necklace . . . colorful dress clips worn at the neck.

· Wear a soft solid-color or dungaree jacket over a Hawaiian shirt; the soft, floppy collar falls nicely over the lapel.

WHERE TO FIND, WHAT TO PAY

As mint-condition Hawaiian shirts become increasingly difficult to find, the market becomes saturated with Hawaiians of poorer quality and prices continue to rise. Keep this in mind when you're searching out Hawaiians. Poor condition means buttonholes may be frayed; buttons may be ripped off, leaving small holes; original wood or coconut buttons may have been replaced with plastic ones; collars may be ragged; fabrics may be worn, faded, or overwashed. Buy the freshest, sturdiest-looking shirt you can find—unless you come across an irresistible print. Then try to bargain and pay less. Try to buy Hawaiian shirts that are 100 percent rayon or cotton, since these fabrics hold up better and can be cared for more easily, either by dry cleaning or hand washing. Wash them in cold water *only*, with cool steam-iron pressing.

A note about buttons: Carved coconut buttons are usually found only on made-in-Hawaii shirts; but it is possible to get coconut (or wood) buttons to replace plastic substitutes. Ask for these where you buy your shirt; vintage shops may have extras to sell you.

Considering how scarce Hawaiian shirts are today, it is surprising how many turn up at vintage shops and flea markets, especially in California. The most beautiful ones, in the best condition, are to be found most easily in New York, Los Angeles, and San Francisco. (For a listing of shops specializing in Hawaiians, see Part Three.)

Vintage Hawaiian shirts can still be found in Hawaii, too. If you're going there on vacation, or know someone who is, check out local sources.

Europeans are so enamored of Hawaiians that they are turning up, surprisingly, in Italy, France, and Holland—countries that buy a great deal of American vintage clothes. But beware: Prices abroad are much higher than in the States.

How much should you expect to pay for a Hawaiian? Prices vary, depending on fabric, where the shirt was made, condition, and design. In general, expect to pay about $85 in the East for a Hawaiian shirt that's collectible (i.e., in good condition and well designed). Prices are higher on the West Coast, and the same shirt will cost you about $95. Anything in silk is now over $100, as are most Japanese-motif shirts. And forties Hawaiian-made crepes (in either rayon or silk) may run as high as $140.

Tuxedos, Silks, Collarbands: Men's Shirting, 1900–1950s

The craze for men's cotton tuxedo-front shirts made from 1900 to the 1950s seems to have passed. *Vogue* magazine showed them for women in 1978, and Saks Fifth Avenue featured them the same year. I've always felt that one should wear a "look" that everyone else is wearing either the year before it becomes the fashion or four years later. To me, that's style. So if you have an old cotton tuxedo shirt, don't throw it away. Now is the time to wear it again. But wear it *differently*. For example: It will look newer worn under a V-neck cashmere sweater, with a cameo or Victorian pin at the neck. Or wear it belted over pants . . . in summer, with the sleeves rolled, over anything white . . . as a beach dress, with flat espadrilles and big gold hoop earrings. They make great nightshirts, too!

You should have little trouble finding a tuxedo shirt in good condition, since they were so seldom worn.

Men's silk collarband shirts made from 1900 to 1950, exceptionally popular with both men and women, are timeless fashion. Keep your eye out for three-ply, white silk tuxedo-front shirts, circa 1920; thirties striped silk shirts, in colors such as black and navy pinstripes on cream (see Norman

Stevens in one on page 85); short-sleeved sports shirts in iridescent pongee, from 1940; men's Chinese silk pajamas, from the fifties (the tops make great shirts); simple muslin baker's shirts; and heavy cotton *grand-pères*.

Special detailing to look for: embroidered sleeve initials, contrasting piping on pajama tops, patch pockets, and jacquard fabrics.

Many vintage men's shirts made between 1900 and 1940 had separate collars. Most have been lost in the recycling. If you don't like the collarless style, a new collar can easily be made; ask a dressmaker or men's custom shirtmaker such as Brooks Brothers. But a lot of men and women like wearing collarless—collarband—shirts either open at the neck or closed with studs, pins, or ribbon ties.

HOW TO WEAR SILK AND COLLARBAND SHIRTS

- For women, collarband silk shirts can be paired with skirts, pants, or suits. They can be casual, worn with a tweed jacket and wool pants. Or they can be slipped under a crepe or velvet jacket or a sequined sweater for evening.
- Another look: a silk tuxedo shirt with a pair of black satin-striped tuxedo pants and a sequined forties jacket. Accessories: pearls or French paste jewelry.
- For day I wear a fifties printed silk shirt with a hand-knitted Scottish Fair Isle vest and Harris tweed pants. The printed shirt, patterned sweater, and tweed pants work well together even though each garment is patterned, because the predominant colors of each are brown, beige, and red.
- Actor Robert Christian owns six vintage silk shirts—all solid-colored, in shades such as mint green, beige, ecru—and stores them in individual plastic bags. He wears them for evening or for day, with jeans—the mainstay of his wardrobe—and sleeves rolled, for a more casual look. For accessories, Robert adds cowboy boots and a tooled-leather belt; or, for a more pulled-

Robert Christian, the actor, collects fine old silk shirts. Here is one of his favorites: a heavy silk tuxedo shirt worn as a jacket, with sleeves rolled, over a silk T-shirt and pleated pants.

Right: *Two black rayon bowling shirts with machine embroidery—worn with jeans here and often paired with painter's pants or khaki twill pants.*

Below: *Striped silk collarband shirt worn with tails out over cotton-twill jodhpurs. Flat leather moccasins complete the casual outfit.*

together look, he wears forties white suede wingtip shoes.

· If your man's silk shirt has an attached collar, it will look good with any kind of tie. Best bet for a very small-collared shirt: a vintage silk bowtie.

WHERE TO FIND, WHAT TO PAY

Men's silk and cotton shirts from the forties and fifties are easier to find in vintage-clothing shops than those made during the twenties and thirties. As a general rule, the silk and older cotton shirts are the most expensive. Expect to pay between $30 and $45 for cotton collarband shirts and $80 and up for silk versions.

A Few Words About Bowling Shirts

One of the most interesting shirts around is the slightly "punk" bowling shirt from the fifties and sixties, made in rayon gabardine or cotton for both men and women and worn by members of bowling teams during tournament play. Most have the bowler's first name (e.g., Betty Lou, Doris, or Stanley) embroidered on the front pocket; others have the team insignia. The ones to look for are those with the most amusing sponsors or slogans embroidered in script across the back. The best bowling shirt I ever sold was inscribed "Bowl with Jesus."

Care of Men's Shirts

RAYON GABARDINE

Many of my customers wash their rayon-gabardine shirts; but this can leave them faded. And ironing can leave a sheen on the fabric. I recommend having rayon gabardine dry-cleaned, especially if it's a printed fabric (because dyes could run all over each other). Dry cleaning also gives vintage shirts, especially the older ones, a fresher, pressed look.

If you insist on hand washing, use *cool* water, mild soap, Wisk for extra-dirty necklines and cuffs, and rinse well. Always iron the shirt with steam and set the regulating button on WOOL. To avoid adding a sheen to the shirt, put a towel between the iron and the shirt.

If you decide to dry-clean your shirt, request that sleeves be pressed without a crease and that the pocket flaps be pressed separately.

HAND WASHING HAWAIIAN SHIRTS

1. Wash shirt in cold water and Woolite.
2. Rinse well.
3. Hang to dry on plastic (not wire) hanger.
4. When the shirt is nearly dry but still damp to the touch, press it with an iron set on a very cool setting, with steam.

SILK SHIRTS

Dry cleaning is recommended for all silk shirts, especially those with tuxedo fronts, because pressing them is difficult. A solid-colored pongee shirt can be washed gently. Use tepid water, with Ivory flakes, then rinse thoroughly; dry on a plastic hanger. Pongee fabric dries quickly and irons easily with a steam iron.

If you purchase a vintage silk shirt that is stained, and dry cleaning does not work, try soaking the shirt overnight in a sinkful of tepid water with a half-cup of well-dissolved Snowy or Clorox Two bleach. In the morning rinse the shirt thoroughly, allow it to dry, and then examine it. If the stains remain, repeat the process using *slightly* more bleach. But remember: These bleaches are very hard on silk fibers; you are shortening the life of your shirt.

11

Sweaters: Vintage Values

The best reasons to buy vintage sweaters: They're often hand knitted, reasonably priced, and uniquely detailed—and they're better "buys" than most sweaters sold today.

Hand- and machine-knitted vintage sweaters, mostly from the forties and fifties, are available at antique-clothing boutiques, flea markets, and house sales. Your mother (or grandmother) may even have one tucked away that she made for you when you were a teenager. Get it out; it will probably fit—sweaters were knitted a little big in those days.

Cashmere Sweaters

Don't ever throw out a well-made cashmere sweater in good condition—that is, one with no moth holes or matted underarms. If you find one you like for sale at an antique-clothing shop, buy it; the price will be right, because new cashmere can only get more expensive, not less. The reason: 100 percent virgin cashmere is made of the soft undercoat fleece of the Kashmir goat, either picked off thorny bushes high in the mountains of Mongolia and China, collected from the ground, or combed from the chest and belly of the goat, then cleaned and sterilized. Collecting cashmere is a tedious job. You can imagine what a herder's fingers must look like after picking enough goat hairs to make one sweater! Unfortunately, there aren't going to be many people around who want to do this kind of work much longer.

My mother sent me off to college with eighteen cashmere sweaters—all bought on sale in Philadelphia department stores. Some were lost while I was in college; others I gave away. I was left with three.

Years later I was buying vintage clothing in a Connecticut flea market and digging—unsuccessfully—into baskets of sweaters mixed with linens

and hankies, when I felt I was about to make a "hit." I can feel it in my bones when I'm about to turn up a treasure. Finally, I came up with a ribbed camel-colored sweater that seemed familiar. A label on the inside read "pure cashmere"; another read "Harriet R. Love." I bought my own sweater—still in my wardrobe, still wearable—for two dollars.

When shopping for vintage cashmere, buy the best, usually made in Scotland. Dalton and Ballantyne, for example, are two quality labels.

Cashmere (especially from the forties and fifties) is not only luscious to the touch but warm to wear because it is "triple ply." Forties and fifties cashmere sweaters were made in every color, and color combination, you can imagine. Among my color favorites: charcoal gray with light gray trim; lemon yellow, flower-embroidered with multicolor yarns; hot pink with gold buttons; baby pink or teal blue decorated with white butterflies; and anything in white cashmere.

Cashmere sweaters of the fifties, by the way, have one thing in common: three-quarter sleeves. This should not put you off. It's an attractive detail, with certain advantages: You can show off the cuffs of a blouse or shirt, or bare your wrists—many people find that sexy. In fact, don't be put off by any detail that is not the current fashion.

Some are not only charming, but they could—and often do—show up in next year's clothes.

HOW TO WEAR CASHMERES

Wear cashmeres over a silk blouse, with matching pants . . . tucked into pants . . . belted over jeans or leather pants . . . under a tweed suit jacket instead of a blouse . . . with tailored flannel pants or wool skirts. Another pretty look: a cashmere cardigan reversed and buttoned down the back,

---

Top left: *A hand-knitted man's Fair Isle vest, so called because of the multicolored intricate patterning of Shetland wools originating on Fair Isle, of Scotland. This one was made in the 1930s. See page 116 for how women can wear them.*

Top right: *A one-of-a-kind 1930s machine-knitted rayon sweater in red with black stripes and red appliquéd zigzags across the chest. This uniquely designed sweater is tucked into new black cashmere pants; the belt—antelope and sterling silver from the 1950s. Handmade old and new—mixed for a totally contemporary look.*

Opposite: *Nina Malkin is wearing a rare 1940s bouclé sweater from my collection; a gray-brown, hand-knitted wool, geometrically patterned with clear crystal beads. The pattern was not applied but knitted in with the bouclé. Even the buttons are bouclé and beads.*

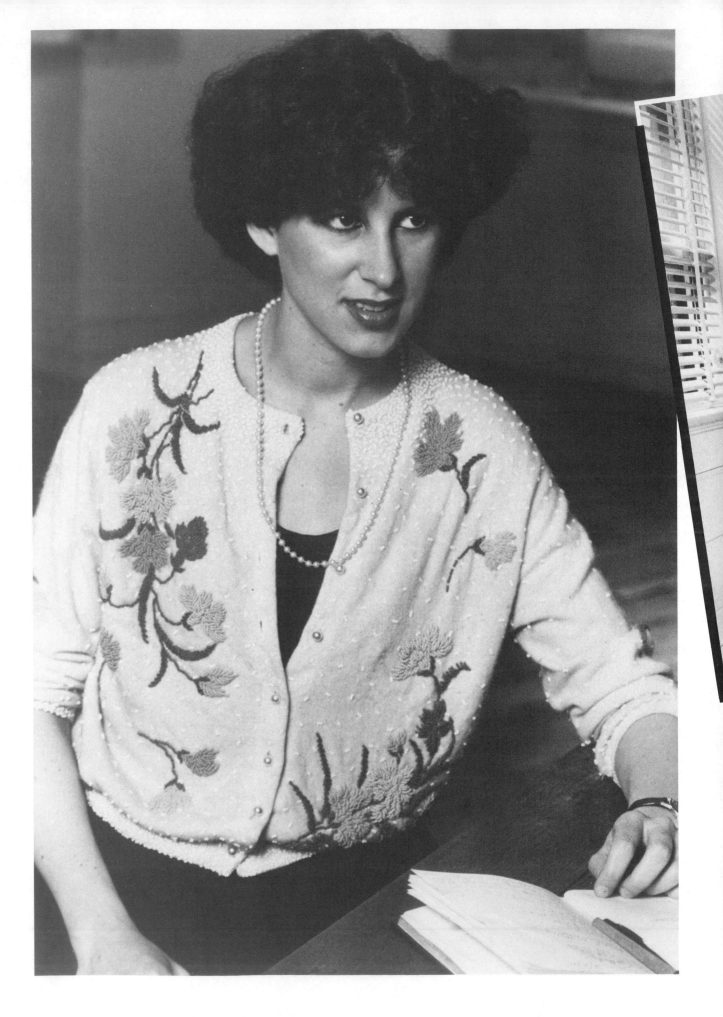

with linen or wool pants or Bermudas. Try tucking a cashmere sweater into a skirt or a pair of pants and adding a suede belt in a bright or contrasting color. Wear a red cashmere cardigan, for instance, over a contrasting pullover to create a different-looking sweater set (great-looking over a pair of black leather pants). You'll get versatility out of pale sherbet colors, such as melon, and neutrals like navy and tan.

Fair Isle Sweaters

Another sweater collector's favorite is the multicolored Fair Isle, in vest, cardigan, or pullover styles. The vest is the most commonly found style. Vests are a favorite of both men and women and can be worn comfortably over gabardine or button-down cotton shirts with jeans and a tweed jacket.

I found my best Fair Isle knits in the late sixties and early seventies in England and Scotland, where they were handmade with as many as fifteen colors of pure Shetland wool. Today, Fair Isles in good condition are hard to find. Alternatives include buying expensive copies or hand knitting them yourself. If you can live with a few moth holes, you can still find Fair Isles in London antique markets.

Bouclé Knits

Bouclé knits, which are made of a nubby, thick-and-thin yarn, are a special favorite of mine and of many other sweater collectors. They can be hand or machine knitted in rayon, silk, or wool. Much of the bouclé-thread hand knitting was done in the twenties and thirties, although some is still being done. By the forties and fifties bouclé was being machine knitted into suits. The hand-knitted bouclé suits from the forties and fifties—if you can find them—are a prize. Those most valued are hand or custom knitted in multicolors, such as black and white (for a salt-and-pepper effect) or black, white, and red, with beading knitted into the sweater. Especially beautiful and sought after are sweaters with gold and lurex threads knitted in, plus beading. The beading is usually at the collar and cuffs, and sometimes extends part way down the chest of the sweater.

You can also find good-looking machine-knitted

Left: *Janet Siefert in her own favorite beaded cashmere: cream with a multicolored floral design worn with old pearls over a silk T-shirt.*

Above: *This black cap-sleeved bouclé forties sweater has gold and iridescent blue sequins hand applied to the front. It's worn with a black crepe fifties skirt and high heels. It could also work well under a suit jacket.*

Above: *A black lambswool sweater with white pearlized beads knitted in—worn over a white crepe forties blouse and pleated black gabardine pants belted with black lizard.*

Right: *For freedom of movement while roller skating, Hedy Klineman wears a peach body stocking and a short skirt; for glitter, a 1950s sweater sequined all over in iridescent white.*

bouclé sweaters with beading or lurex threads, though they're not as prized as hand- or custom-knitted sweaters. Other machine-made sweaters to look for are those with the Kimberly label. Kimberly (still manufacturing today) made some terrific-looking machine-made bouclé matching sweaters and skirts in the forties and fifties that are still in great shape today.

Always check bouclé-wool sweaters for moth holes and matted underarms—as you would any vintage sweater. Make sure the dressier versions, trimmed with beading and pearls, are in good condition. Check to see if the beading pattern is complete, and ask if the sweater has been dry-cleaned; most beaded sweaters that survive dry cleaning with beading intact are in good shape. (For more about the care of beading, see pages 64–65.)

Sequined and Beaded Sweaters

Another great find: the fifties and sixties sequined or beaded cardigan sweater, usually made in Hong Kong, of lambswool, rabbit's hair, or cashmere (rarer and more expensive). Best in this category are the hand-knitted versions made in Italy, lined in silk, with knitted-in (rather than sewn-on) sequins, in jet black, iridescent white, or light blue. I once had a rare sequined pewter-colored sweater in the store, which a woman bought—and wore out of the store over her gray flannel pants and cream blouse, creating a dazzling evening look.

If you're looking for beaded sweaters, seek out cashmere studded on the yoke with iridescent beading, or with contrasting beading—jet-black beading on red cashmere, for instance, or with

Three ways to wear figuratives: (left) Alexandra Penney wears a "little girl" hand-knitted sweater from the thirties over a thirties rayon print dress (collar out, pearls as accessory); (center) Gina Davis looks casual in machine-made figurative over Hawaiian shirt (collar out) and jeans; (right) Eliot Hubbard wears a classic hand-knitted reindeer cardigan over a shirt and gray cords.

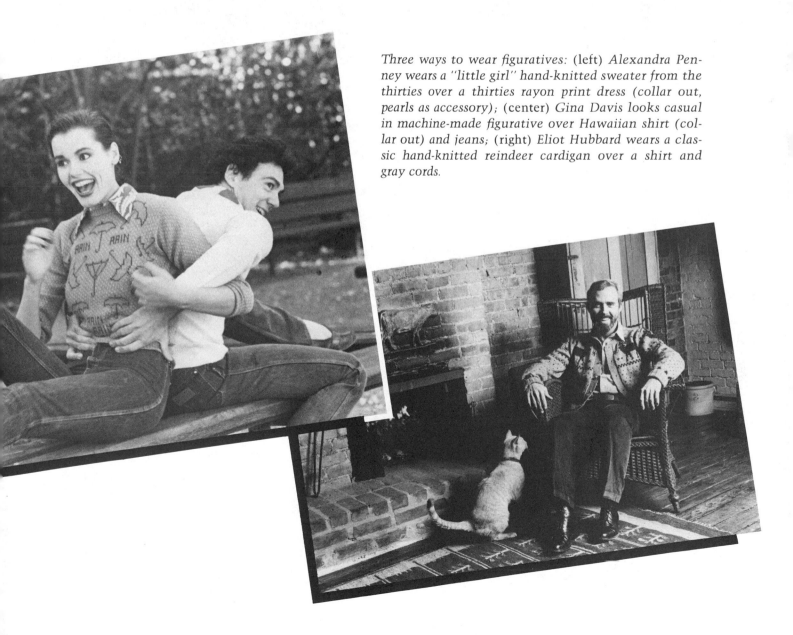

Three 1950s machine-made reindeer figurative sweaters with funky designs: polar bears and penguins in gray, white, and black; snowflakes in red, white, and blue; lips and hearts with the words "sealed with a kiss" and "straight from my heart," in deep purple and white.

matched beading—iridescent on white. Other handsome combinations include pastels: white beading over pale pink cashmere or rabbit's hair; and the most dramatic—caviar beading on black cashmere. All these combinations of beading and sequins can be worn with the same color pants, silk or linen skirts, or over a silk shirt as a jacket.

A note on care: *Always* have sequined or beaded sweaters dry-cleaned. For more about the care of beading, see pages 64–65.

Figuratives

Bulky sweaters of the forties and fifties with hand-made figurative designs, always favorites with customers, are big sellers. The best have bowling or golfing motifs; some have a big eagle on the back or an American Indian design. You can also find football players, old cars, and pine trees.

Another category of handmade figuratives is what I call the "little-girl" wool sweaters of the thirties and forties. They are cable- or rib-knitted and embroidered with flowers, animals, and people along the front, back, pockets, and cuffs. Often these sweaters tie at the neck with wool ties finished at the ends with little wool balls. If you find one of these treasures, buy it and wear it like a jacket over blouses and dresses.

One of the most popular styles to collect is the machine-made reindeer, snowflake, or moosehead sweater, all usually referred to as "reindeers." My husband collects these sweaters; he owns two real reindeers, one raindrops figurative, others with lips and an eagle, one with music notes and bars. My own favorite: a handmade figurative done with hearts and flowers.

Caring for Your Sweaters

Some people advise hand washing sweaters; others insist dry cleaning is better. I think the choice is up to you—except if your sweater is beaded or sequined. Then, dry-clean *only*. Dry cleaners point out that even cold water causes wool to shrink slightly. And, of course, it's much less time-consuming (although more expensive) to put your sweaters in the hands of a good cleaner. Those who prefer washing like it because washing makes their sweaters smell nice and also allows them to reblock the sweaters the way they like them each time. As to which process removes spots better, that depends on the type of stain—and the skill of the washer or dry cleaner.

Certain sweaters—embroidered (especially on white wool) and Fair Isle—should be dry-cleaned rather than washed because they have so many colors and are not always colorfast.

If you opt to wash, here's the best way: In a basin filled with about two gallons of cool water, pour one to one-and-a-half capfuls of liquid Woolite. Mix the Woolite thoroughly in the water; use your hands. Then put in one cashmere sweater, squeezing it gently for two or three minutes. If the inner neckline or cuffs are soiled, rub them very gently. Using cool water, rinse the sweater very thoroughly in the same basin. Change the water several times so that you are sure the sweater is completely free of soap. Lay it on a clean towel to dry.

In warm weather, store sweaters in canvas or plastic bags with mothballs.

Prices of Sweaters

Plain cashmere sweaters: $35–$50

Beaded cashmere: $65–$125

Fair Isle; perfect condition and multicolored: $75–$90

Bouclé knits: $40–$90

Sequined cardigan sweaters: $60–$125

Figurative and reindeer sweaters: $45–$150

12

Pants: Super Styles

Pants. You probably own dozens of pairs. And with good reason: Pants are without question the most versatile clothing in a woman's wardrobe today. They are basics—as important to own as a skirt or a jacket; they are "musts." No active woman can live without them—in the country, in the city, for day, for knocking around, for evening, they work for you around the clock. Today, designers include pants in every collection—in almost every style. And as with skirt lengths, anything goes. In any one season you may wear narrow trousers, jodhpurs, tailored men's pleated pants, Zouave pants for evening; and in summer, shorts—from Bermuda length to short shorts. Why? Because they're comfortable. They're stylish. They're easy. And they're versatile. Pants can be dressed up or down just by trading a turtleneck sweater for a camisole or a silk blouse or by adding a different belt, another pair of earrings, or a dressier shoe. Pants can be turned from day to night as easily as that.

And if you shop for pants in vintage-clothing stores, the range of what's available increases. You're going to find more variety in *shape*—everything from full-legged to pencil-slim capri pants; in *style*—from culottes to Bermudas; and *length*—from the shortest shorts to midcalf clam diggers to ankle-long pajamas.

What's going to work best for you from all that's available? Here are the choices.

Forties and Fifties Pleated Pants

Many vintage-clothing stores devote a good portion of their space to men's forties and fifties pleated pants—and both men and women buy them. There is also a vintage version made for women; the difference is in the style; instead of a fly front, it has a side zipper, with a little more hip room and a smaller waistline.

Pleated pants can be found everywhere but especially in New York, Los Angeles, and San Francisco. They come in a wide variety of fabrics: pinstripes, tweeds, linens, flannels, shantung, and gabardine. The rarest, hardest-to-find fabrics are the colorful tweeds, white linen, and black or pink gabardine. These are widely desired, so it is going to take some luck—and some searching—to come up with a pair.

For evening, check out men's black wool tuxedo pants with grosgrain ribbon stripes down the sides. These pleated men's and boys' pants are a great dressy choice. They can be worn with a tuxedo jacket and silk blouse, or they can be paired with a cream silk thirties blouse and marcasite pin or bracelet, as shown on pages 108 and 109.

If you want an idea of how pleated pants should look, watch Katharine Hepburn closely the next time *Pat and Mike* is on television. Hepburn wears pleated-pants-and-sweater outfits that are as contemporary a look as you could find. In fact, almost any sweater or shirt works with pleated pants—they're so basic and so easy to wear. Jane Pauley, of the *Today Show*, recently bought a pair of men's pleated navy gabardine pants from me and wore them into the store the next week with a silk blouse under a cardigan sweater: a very classic, casual look. For a dressier look, wear them with a crepe blouse from the forties that buttons down the back and a bronze-colored leather belt. Both women and men can attractively pair pleated pants with a gab shirt, as shown on page 109.

One problem you will probably encounter: a low crotch in both the men's and women's version. This can be easily altered. When you are buying pleated pants, make sure the waist fits; if not, have it taken in. And be sure there is enough length for your taste—men were a little shorter thirty years ago.

The sizes that sell the fastest are waist sizes 28, 29, 30, 31, 32, because these fit both men and women. Larger sizes, such as 33, 34, 35, 36, are always available; they can be altered and are usually reasonably priced. Or buy pleated pants slightly big and belt them for a gathered-waist look à la Annie Hall—especially those in linen, gab, and lightweight rayon.

Two other problems to keep your eye on: Check for moth holes, as you would when buying any vintage-wool clothing. And be sure the pants you're buying are already cleaned and pressed, so that there's less chance of discovering moth holes after you've taken your pants home. The second problem is shine, which occurs from over-cleaning, mostly in gab fabrics. Not much can be done about shine, which affects appearance but not condition.

Pajama Pants

One item coveted by those who have discovered their comfort and versatility are men's pajama bottoms in a silk or cotton. Women wear them in summer for evening, while men pray they can find the tops so they can sleep in them. (Bottoms are easier to find than tops—don't ask me why.) Men's PJs have a drawstring or elastic waist and come in a range of classic colors—cream, burgundy, pale blue, navy, and white. Some, in silk, have a jacquard-weave pattern; most have contrasting colored trim or piping around the cuff and up the side. I once owned a pair custom-made from Sulka: all-white silk with a jacquard weave of champagne bottles and bubbles—gorgeous!

Three years ago I bought a pair of white cotton PJs, originally sold by Brooks Brothers in the fifties, which I wear over bathing suits, with rolled-up cuffs to show more ankle, and flat sandals or beach shoes. Another way to wear PJs is with matching stockings and high-heel sandals or pumps. If your "pants" are white, match up stockings to shoes rather than to pants.

Men's PJs are usually sized A, B, C, and D; A is the smallest size. Sometimes these "pants" are shorter than you are accustomed to wearing, but that should never stop you from purchasing them—pants can be worn in *all* lengths. For example, if you find a pair you love that are too short, make them *shorter*; make them into real clam diggers. Or Bermudas. They don't always have to reach below the ankle.

Before buying silk pajama pants, inspect them carefully by holding them up to the light. This will give you a better picture of their condition. Don't forget that pajama pants were worn a lot and washed frequently.

You may come across some women's trousers made in men's PJ style that date from the twenties

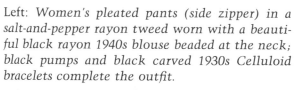

Left: Women's pleated pants (side zipper) in a salt-and-pepper rayon tweed worn with a beautiful black rayon 1940s blouse beaded at the neck; black pumps and black carved 1930s Celluloid bracelets complete the outfit.

Below: Dark green, cuffed gabardine pleated pants with attached leopard belt loops—worn with matching opaque stockings and shoes and a chartreuse Hawaiian shirt.

Three different outfits built around one pair of black wool boy's tuxedo pants with grosgrain ribbon side stripes: (left) with 1930s silk-chiffon blouse, bar pin, black satin-brocade vest, and bronze leather belt; (center) with same chiffon blouse, same belt (one in red satin would also work well), bar pin, and satin pumps; (right) with chiffon blouse, Deco necklace, charcoal gray pin-striped jacket, and suede striped gloves.

Above: Pleated pants go well with gab shirts and can be belted in a variety of inventive ways, from alligator skin to narrow silk scarves.

through the fifties. These were often paired with Chinese-style tops. If you're lucky, you can find the sets; more often you can only find pants. The more elaborate pairs are of jacquard silk, with embroidered cuffs and elastic waistbands. The blouses have embroidered pockets and sleeves. Originally intended as lounging outfits, they make great-looking evening separates. The extra plus: They are often found unworn in their original gift box. (It seems no one used to wear gifts from Japan or China.)

Pajama-style pants were also made by American companies in colorful stripes, Japanese and Hawaiian prints, and "little girl" motifs such as pink sheep floating in the sky among blue clouds. Most of these pants were made of rayon and held up well through many washings. Many of my customers wear them with halters, cotton T-shirts, or bandeaus for summer. Others have worn them with men's silk shirts—belted and bloused over the pants.

Capri Pants, Clam Diggers, and Bermudas

Fifties pants in shorter lengths—fitted capris, knee-length clam diggers, and Bermudas—are turning up in vintage-clothing boutiques and have become a familiar sight on summer streets. The fitted capri style—with its ankle length and tighter leg bottoms—goes well with a strapless top, tank top, or T-shirt and flat shoes for a casual look. For a dressier version, try high mules. Bermudas and clam diggers are fun to wear with striped cotton boys' shirts, belted Hawaiian shirts, and colorful boat-neck T-shirts. Most shorter pants look best with flat sandals, which add comfort to a casual look. Some women also wear capris (or clam diggers) under full skirts, a great effect if you can pull it off—if colors mix well and everything (hair, makeup, accessories) works stylishly together. One note: Shorter, tighter pants are not for everybody. Your best accessory for skin-tight clothes is a body in shape!

Country Riding Pants

I don't think any of us can quite forget our Western heroes or their unique fashion style, because I

Two pairs of printed rayon pajama pants—one with an oriental motif, the other with a floral—worn on the right with a crocheted bathing-suit top and above with a scarf tied around the bosom.

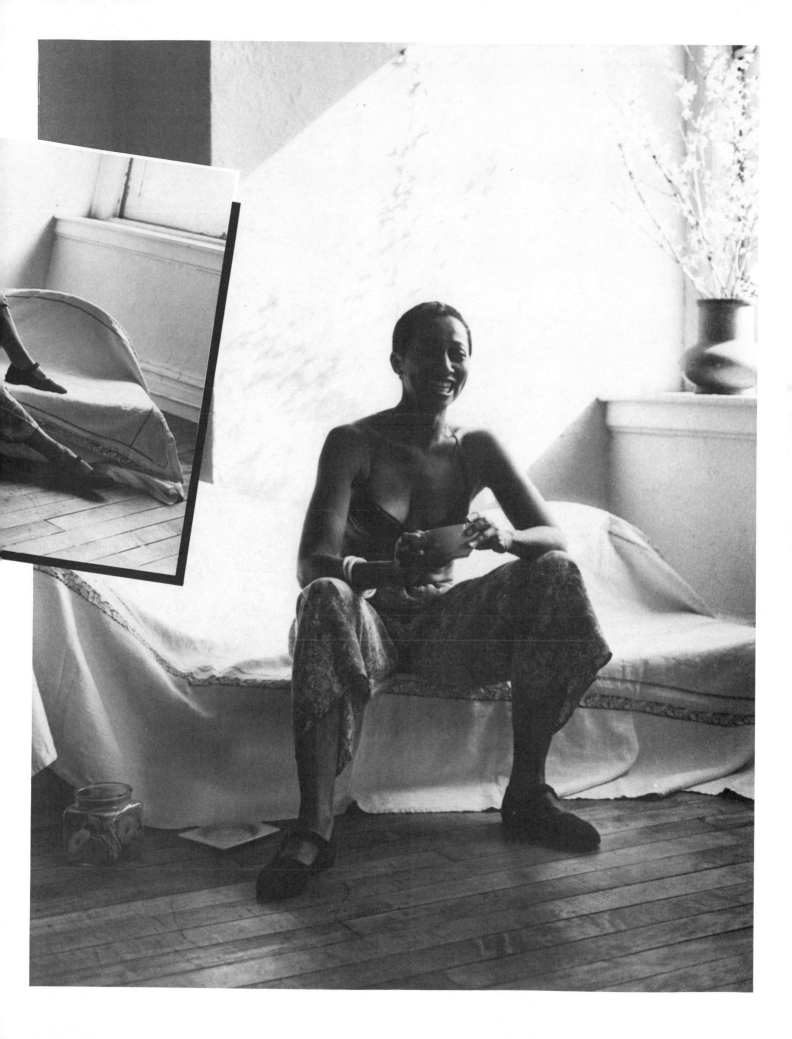

have never been able to keep a pair of chaps, linen breeches, traditional jodhpurs, or rodeo pants in my store for more than a day or two.

Women pair them with a vintage button-down oxford-cloth Brooks Brothers shirt, either solid colored or striped, and a tweed jacket. Men have been seen in linen jodhpurs and silk shirts at summer parties in Southampton. My own favorite winter "uniform": cotton-twill jodhpurs, paired either with a striped button-down Brooks Brothers shirt or a collarless roll-sleeved shirt under a Fair Isle vest or sweater, both always tucked in; accessorized with an interesting belt—either an Indian beaded one or something in snakeskin or canvas.

Skating and Ski Pants

If you ever come across a vintage ski, snow-, or ice-skating suit, don't dally. Buy it—unless you live in the Sun Belt. But if you live where winters are long and cold, you will be the warmest and happiest person on the streets during cold-weather months. These "thermal" pants are usually made of heavy wool on the outside; inside they're lined in cotton flannel, with a stretch waist and cuffed ankle. They look like sweat pants, but they're even warmer. Less warm are the snowsuits made of lightweight rayon or gabardine—sometimes printed with an amusing snowflake pattern. The matching jacket, if you can find it, is worth its weight in gold: Its *reversible* poplin lining is waterproof.

What You Should Expect to Pay

- For pleated pants in tweed, wool, linen, gabardine—cleaned, pressed, without moth holes—expect to pay between $40 and $50. If you don't mind a little shine or a few moth holes, you can get pleated pants for as little as $15 to $20.
- For men's PJs: If you're lucky enough to find them in silk jacquard, you'll pay about $60. Cotton or printed-rayon PJs (in Hawaiian or paisley designs) cost about $35. And anything with Chinese embroidery is about $50. American-made Japanese prints—there are a lot of these around—run about $35. And if you find any PJ pants with their tops, prices will be about double.
- Capris, clam diggers, and Bermudas are easiest to find in shops specializing in fifties clothing, and you should be able to purchase them for under $50.
- Good-condition jodhpur pants—in khaki, black, red, blue, twills, cotton, or corded—cost about $55. Linens, which are older and date from 1900 to 1930, are harder to find and so may be a little more expensive—about $75.
- The average price for a ski suit is about $75.

Left: *Fifties clam diggers worn with a fifties white blouse and late-forties gabardine suit jacket; accessorized with funky ankle socks and men's brown-and-beige shoes.*

Above: *Once worn strictly for country riding, khaki-colored cotton-twill jodhpurs look comfortably sporty here with silk-chiffon embroidered Rumanian blouse and flat shoes.*

13

Skirts: Easy Pieces

Skirts can add versatility to your wardrobe; yet as versatile as they are, they can also add confusion. A dress is a dress is a dress—you put it on, add a belt, and you are "dressed." But wearing a skirt, a vintage one at that, means putting it together with other pieces for a total look. The question always arises: What do you pair with it? Once you have built a basic wardrobe of vintage blouses, camisoles, jackets, and sweaters, it is easy to wear these basic vintage tops with vintage skirts. Victorian skirts are very long; twenties skirts are shorter; in the thirties skirts were long again; the forties and fifties went from short to long; by the sixties skirts were up to the midthigh. All these skirt lengths are available to you. But you don't have to keep vintage skirts at their original length either. You can alter lengths to meet your needs, to the proportion that looks best on you.

Victorian/Edwardian Skirts and Petticoats

Old Victorian and Edwardian skirts and petticoats can be found in quilted wool and cotton, embroidered satins, and brocaded silks. They can be ankle length and ruffled on the bottom with a fitted waist that ties in the back. The gathered fitted waist, elaborate fabrics, and full lengths are elegant.

Finding the kind of Victorian and Edwardian skirt that is wearable today is not so easy. Fabrics are eighty to a hundred years old, so skirts in good or wearable condition are hard to come by. And styles are full, long, and cumbersome. But all is not lost! Each item of clothing, whether elaborate or simple, has its appropriate occasion. Here are some possibilities for buying and wearing the impossible skirt.

Although long Victorian and Edwardian skirts and silk petticoats were originally made to wear with taffeta, velvet, brocade, and satin bodices or

115

Left: *This all-cotton petticoat with its hand-done embroidery and openwork, purchased at a French flea market, is a perfect example of an Edwardian petticoat that is suitably worn as a skirt. Here with a boy's cotton shirt, a Fair Isle vest, a netted-lace bow at the neck, and cowboy boots.*

Below: *A perfectly beautiful black background, printed skirt cut from a forties dress. The waistband was made from the bodice, and a new zipper was put in. It is worn here with lizard shoes and a black crepe blouse that has rhinestone-trimmed cuffs.*

blouses, most people today prefer to mix rather than match. Example: A long, full Victorian skirt in brown taffeta works beautifully with an embroidered-crepe folkloric blouse from the thirties. An Edwardian pongee skirt, trimmed with black velvet, could be teamed with a forties black velvet jacket. A crochet-edged, ankle-length linen skirt looks good, for instance, with a cap-sleeved cream-colored bouclé sweater.

If you love Victorian/Edwardian petticoats, try this: Make an Edwardian-type skirt—with all its eyelet, lace, and embroidery—from a white-cotton or linen christening gown. Christening gowns are a lot easier to find than adult-size dresses, since there isn't much use for them after a christening. The length of fabric from the waist down is often long enough to convert into an adult-size skirt, and the gathering will expand to accommodate an adult waist. A simple waistband (using ribbon or white cotton fabric) is easy to make—even for a nonsewer. And christening clothes are much less expensive than women's petticoats: A box of christening dresses (not all elaborate and not all in perfect condition) was sold at a recent auction for $50.

Skirts from the Thirties, Forties, and Fifties

The best printed skirts found in vintage-clothing boutiques are made from large-size vintage rayon and silk dresses that are not salable—either because they are very big or because the top is not in good condition. To turn a dress into a skirt, it's not necessary to cut a pattern; just take the top of the dress off at the waistline. Gather the skirt to fit your waist, put in a side zipper, and cut a one-inch waistband from the top part of the dress. There are lots of seams, darts, and sleeves to deal with when cutting a waistband in this way; so if you're not a good sewer, give this project to a seamstress. Even with this extra expense, the skirt will still be cheaper than a new one. And you will have a more interesting skirt in fabric and detail, too.

Pleated Skirts

Pleated skirts are always on their way in or out—depending on whether clothes are leaning toward

a fuller or straighter look. If you run across pleated skirts from any era buy them and keep them *forever* . . . they are bound to be back in fashion soon. Even if they aren't, you can create your own style with a pleated skirt. A circle of pleats, straight pleats, or pleats that start at the hip all offer a fresh-but-classic look. If you still have your pleated plaid college skirt, take it out and create your own "suit" for day with a blazer. For evening, look for pleated taffeta or crepe skirts to wear with a bare camisole or a fitted strapless bustier.

Hand-Painted Mexican Full Skirts

If you've seen the movie *Grease*, you know what a "circle skirt" is. This style was usually trimmed with designs such as poodles, umbrellas, or fruit—all great-looking but most too dated for today. Much more flattering and appealing to wear are the hand-painted and hand-sequined Mexican circle skirts made in the forties and fifties. Sometimes the skirt is painted in a "primitive" style with people and flowers; sometimes it is decorated with rows of sequins in a geometric design. These Mexican full skirts are found more frequently in antique-clothing shops on the West Coast. When I've had them in my New York shop, they have been hard to sell—except to Europeans who did not think of them as ethnic or folk costumes. A Mexican circle skirt in my collection is hand painted in black and white, with rays of silver sequins in a sunburst pattern (see page 117). I always wear it with the simplest T-shirt or a black body stocking.

Embroidered Chinese Skirts

Embroidered silk Chinese skirts (made in two equal sections held together by a six-inch muslin wrap waistband) were originally worn by Chinese men and women in the nineteenth and early twentieth centuries. The heavily embroidered panels hang in the front and back and the pleating falls to the sides when this skirt is wrapped around the hips.

Embroidered Chinese skirts are becoming harder to find in the United States, except at important clothing auctions and fine antique-clothing bou-

tiques. Some people have found these skirts in Hong Kong; and if you travel, this is a good example of the kind of vintage clothing to look for on the road.

Embroidered Chinese skirts are always needle-worked by hand in colorful silk threads on a jacquard-silk ground. A beautiful example, which recently sold at auction for $600, was described in the auction brochure as "an apron skirt of red satin, with multicolored narrow silk panels, embroidered with colorful silks, and gilded with a full-faced, five-clawed dragon, surrounded by embroidery birds, bats, and cloud scrolls, with multicolored waves swirling below."

The one I own has brass bells attached to ribbonlike pieces that hang from the sides of the skirt. It is shown on page 120.

To wear these skirts properly, wrap the skirt around your waist as you would a towel and then pin at the side to hold the skirt in place. Fold over the six-inch muslin waistband so that less muslin shows.

Short solid-colored tunic tops or Chinese jackets also in solid colors are elegant with these elaborate skirts, and they don't take away from the intricate embroidery.

Another idea to try: Wear a simple but elegant camisole or silk blouse tucked into the muslin waistband, then wrap the waist with a silk fabric cummerbund to cover the muslin. Use a color that matches the blouse or choose the background

Top left: *Pleated skirts in wool, silk, or cotton are forever coming into or going out of style. So it's always safe to have one around in a plaid or solid color. Here a fifties plaid wool is worn in a simple but classic and contemporary way with a bloused wool sweater and a tooled belt with a silver buckle.*

Top right: *A Mexican circle skirt in my collection is hand painted in black and white, with rays of silver sequins in a sunburst pattern. I always wear it with the simplest low-cut T-shirt or a black body stocking.*

Bottom: *This one-of-a-kind tiered, pleated skirt from the 1940s is made of iridescent mauve, celery, and blue taffeta. From the waist to the thigh it consists of fitted black taffeta. It could be worn with a black strapless bustier and wide belt or perhaps a black matte-jersey blouse.*

color of the skirt. Be sure the waistline does not appear too bulky.

Always look for unfaded silks in good condition. Check that the embroidery is intact and that you have both panels on a skirt. The skirt will not wrap properly around the hips if you have only one panel. Dry-clean only.

Suit Skirts

The problem that usually occurs with suit jackets often happens with suit skirts: They are found and sold separately in vintage-clothing boutiques. The advantage is that you don't have to buy a two-piece suit if you only want separates. And if you really want a suit look, you can mix and match to create your own suit from the blazers that you already own or from the vast selection of vintage suit jackets that can be found (see chapter 14). Another advantage to buying skirts and jackets separately is sizing. Many suit jackets appear to be a size smaller than their matching skirt—a size 8 skirt is often paired with a size 6 jacket. Perhaps suit manufacturers in the thirties and forties made odd-sized suits to compensate for women's larger hips and smaller busts.

But, by all means, if you see a gabardine suit that fits and looks great, buy it, and wear it as separates, too. Here's what to look for in suit skirts: a basic full flannel skirt; a dressy and fashionable silk-taffeta skirt with black and pink stripes; a rusty-red or sea-blue knitted skirt (good for work and sexy); a brown, black, and white tweed straight skirt (also good for work); a gored burgundy or black rayon-velvet skirt for parties. All of these styles are probably suit skirts made during the thirties to fifties. Lengths can vary from the knee to the ankle.

Hand-knitted suit skirts from the thirties through the fifties are very wearable if they are properly blocked by a cleaner. Some are knitted in multicolored tweed bouclés; others have metallic threads knitted throughout—bits of gold, silver, or copper, which add a touch of glitter and uniqueness to what ordinarily would be a tailored style. Gold, silver, or copper thread can make a knitted suit skirt look dressy—especially if it is paired with a metallic halter top and jacket.

If you asked ten women what they would wear with a tan or white skirt of linen or gabardine, you would get ten different answers. Some would wear an unconstructed jacket as a summer blazer to create a suit look; others would wear the same skirt every other day with a different T-shirt or blouse. Another person might pair the skirt with a lacy ruffle-edged blouse. In the mid-sixties I found fifty white rayon suits that were made for military women during World War II. I'm not sure what occasions they were worn for, but they were the best-made suits I ever had in quantity in my store. The sizes were confusing: I had eight size 32 jackets—but no size 32 skirts; lots of size 36 skirts but no matching jackets. Instead of trying to match sizes, I sold every piece separately. Some women grabbed up the white jackets; others bought the simple gored white skirts. It was clear summer had begun: Everyone wanted white skirts, and the prices were right. One of my customers wore her outfit into the store before a dinner engagement.

Around her white suit skirt she had pulled together a black outfit. She had on a small-brimmed black straw hat, crocheted black thirties gloves, and a black silk-chiffon blouse with a small lace collar, closed at the neck with a carved mother-of-pearl pin. The effect was striking. I can never associate those skirts with the military again.

Printed Cotton Dirndl Skirts

Wearing a pure-cotton skirt in summer, with bare legs and sandals, is one of the coolest ways to make it through a hot city day. The cotton dirndl skirts designed in the fifties for dancing at the hop, walking along the boardwalk, or meeting a date for a soda can be updated and worn now. The fitted waists, bright colors, and lengths—from just below the knee to above the ankle—make for breezy dressing. Background colors include black, turquoise, white, red, and sometimes cornflower blue or navy, in solids or prints. One favorite,

Far left: *A one-of-a-kind late–1940s skirt that doesn't fit into any "category": black silk-velvet midcalf skirt with red, green, and gold bands that fall into a chevron pattern. The beautifully patterned skirt dances as the bias-cut velvet moves. Lovely worn with a short black velvet jacket.*

Center: *This red silk Chinese apron skirt has blue, turquoise, lavender, pink, gray, and cream embroidery on its front and back panels. At the bottom are brass bells and a colorful silk fringe attached to ribbons of embroidery. It looks very elegant worn with a royal blue Chinese-style jacket or long-sleeved silk tunic reaching the hip bone.*

Left: *A black cotton dirndl skirt with an aqua, hot pink, putty, and purple dock scene depicting beach, boats, people, and a quaint old town. All pulled together with a new belted, black cotton sweater.*

Below: *A copper-colored, hand-knitted bouclé suit skirt, which originally came with a matching bouclé sweater that was probably decorated with real copper threads. This one is being paired with an almost matching rust bouclé knitted top.*

done in pink, blue, orange, chartreuse, and white chrysanthemums, has Chinese men and women floating down a river in sampans, all on a black background (shown on this page). Another is also on a black ground, with an aqua, hot-pink, putty, and purple dock scene, depicting beach, boats, people, and a quaint old town.

Prices

Here's roughly what you can expect to pay for vintage skirts, depending on age, condition, and detailing.

Victorian skirts and petticoats: $50–$200
Printed rayon or silk skirts: $40–$65
Pleated skirts in wool and rayon: $40–$75
Mexican painted and sequined skirts: $75–$150
Embroidered Chinese skirts: $150–$800
Suit skirts: $25–$50
Cotton dirndl skirts: $35–$60

14

Jackets and Blazers: Seasonless Dressing

There is hardly a person around who cannot look through his or her wardrobe and find one or two jackets that can be worn any day, any season. Jackets are a must to own—for adding or removing with a change of weather, for turning a day look into evening look or vice versa. A dressy jacket can be worn over everything—over a dress, over a sweater and a skirt, over pants and a pretty blouse. Vintage jackets have the plus of being less expensive than newer versions. And vintage jackets from the twenties through the fifties can be found in abundance in vintage-clothing boutiques. (One exception: For comfort's sake, avoid Victorian jackets. Although they are beautiful and made of beaded silks, wools, and linens, their tight armholes, high-boned necks, and bodices make them uncomfortable to wear.)

Evening and Dressy Jackets

Asymmetric designs . . . bias cutting . . . flowing sleeves . . . "Chanel" styling, with long waists—or none at all . . . glorious velvets, lamés, beading, sequins—that's what's available. The best jackets to buy and wear are those made of the most extraordinary fabrics, such as panne velvet in colors like peach, purple, or mint green, or flocked multicolored velvets with silver and gold threads running through them in swirling floral designs. Also prized are silkscreened Art Deco printed jackets in pale colors with fuchsia, green, or black floral prints; and, of course, jackets covered in sequins. A standout in my collection is a twenties jacket covered in silver sequins, open to the hip, where it closes with a rhinestone clasp. It was meant to be worn over a dress. I wear it with a camisole, underslip, or slip dress. Many years ago, I rented it to someone who wore it with a strapless black satin bodysuit, black ankle-strap shoes, and rhinestone drop earrings. That was all! Another treasure: a forties black wool jacket with sequins

worked in a geometric design, with a high collar, hourglass bodice, and long, fitted sleeves. I wear it with black wool tuxedo pants, velvet capri pants, or a bias-cut velvet skirt.

A note about beaded or sequined jackets: Most of those available will be from the forties and fifties and should be in excellent condition. Often they are lined in colorful silks or rayons. Sometimes the colors of the beading on collars and pockets will contrast with the wool gabardine or crepe of the jacket. Or sometimes iridescent beading (often called carnival glass) of the same color will be used.

Styling varies: Forties and fifties jackets can be either full in the back, with a gathered yoke and very full sleeves, or the shape might be very fitted, with padded shoulders and perhaps some shoulder beading. Gabardine was a favorite fabric for these jackets, in shades of deep blue, rust, copper, gray, or black, and occasionally red. Incidentally, most of these decorated jackets were parts of suits that came with simple straight skirts; but most likely you will find the jacket without the skirt, which gives you the option of wearing it your own way. There are no limitations. With a black wool jacket, pick a contrasting velvet skirt or cream-colored wool pants. Choose gray pants with a pewter-beaded jacket, brown suede pants with a copper-beaded jacket.

CONDITION

Always check jacket linings to see that they are clean, untorn, unfaded, and not pulling at the sleeve or hem. Look for unworn sleeve edges: check for moth holes. Make sure the gabardine is not faded at the shoulder and that shoulder pads are not slipping. If a few beads are not in place, have them secured by a seamstress.

Left: A 1930s hip-length lamé jacket with high collar, wrap style, and a capelike swing to the back. Worn in this early photo over a gown.

Right: A 1940s burgundy wool jacket encrusted on the collar with black jet beading. Notice the side closing and well-padded shoulders. It is worn here with new jodhpurlike trousers and pumps.

Right: *A beautiful, original Adrian black gabardine suit jacket, worn here over a 1960s tweed suit skirt.*

Below: *This fitted plaid forties suit jacket seems to have been designed with a Victorian silhouette in mind. It looks wonderful here with a straight suit skirt and riding-style felt hat.*

WHAT YOU SHOULD EXPECT TO PAY

If you find a beaded or sequined jacket in excellent condition, or a very dressy lamé, or a flocked-velvet-and-chiffon jacket, be prepared to pay about $150 and up. Three-quarter-length lamé jackets trimmed with fur will cost around $250. Famous designer names, such as Fortuny, will cost $500 and up. A jacket lightly trimmed with beading—over the bustline or around the cuff or collar, for example—will cost considerably less than $150, about $85.

Daytime Suit Jackets

It's hard to resist the variety of stylish and finely detailed jackets that are available from suits of the thirties through the fifties. Vintage-clothing stores usually have a good selection. The styling might be man-tailored with notched wide lapels or femininely detailed with rhinestone buttons and bows. The jacket may have padded shoulders or raglan sleeves and come in anything from gray wool flannel to red or salmon gabardine, from wool tweeds and herringbones to cream-colored linen or sharkskins, or navy crepe. Details include self-belts, braid-trimmed or embroidered collars and cuffs, touches of beading or fur trim, and asymmetrical closings down the front. The length will go from hip length (sometimes with a peplum) to thigh length. Some will be full backed, some will be fitted.

FIT

The key to finding the right jacket for you is fit. Don't be embarrassed to try on every jacket in a shop. The following tips will help you to get the proper fit:

· The shoulder line (padded or not) should be at your shoulder.
· Unless a jacket is designed with a three-quarter sleeve, the sleeve should come to your wrist. Sleeve lengths can be altered. Shortening is easier than lengthening, because cuffs tend to fray and show wear.
· A long jacket that ends at the thigh is the wrong proportion for a short person. By the same token, a skimpy or very short-waisted

jacket is wrong for a tall woman. Look for proportion and length relative to your body shape. You have thirty years of jackets to choose from!
· Bustlines on vintage jackets were often cut fuller than those being made today. Large-busted women will have a field day. Small-busted women can have their jackets fitted by a good tailor. This added cost is worthwhile when you consider the moderate price of most vintage jackets in comparison to new ones of the same quality.

CARE . . . CONDITION

Most jackets from the thirties through the fifties were made of silk, wool, or rayon. Examine wool jackets carefully for moth holes before making a purchase. One small hole in an inconspicuous place should not spoil a purchase; more than that will give the jacket a shabby appearance. Be sure to look over dark jackets carefully; dark colors make moth holes difficult to detect.

Watch out for frayed or worn cuffs, elbows, and necklines, especially on gabardine or cashmere jackets. Always buy gabardine suit jackets that have no shine on the fabric. (Shine comes from too much wear and pressing.) Make sure underarms are not discolored.

After you have checked the outside of the jacket, it's time to look at the lining. If you love the jacket, it is worth replacing a lining that is torn, faded, or strained. But relining is expensive; before deciding to reline a suit jacket, make sure it is for you and that you will get lots of wear out of it. Don't reline unless it is required; sometimes the lining is not an integral part of the jacket. I have an exceptional black forties Adrian jacket lined in black crepe. It's classic. Because I want to keep it forever, I cover it with a cotton canvas bag; in summer there are mothballs in all the pockets. Only when the lining starts to deteriorate will I replace it—the jacket deserves this kind of care.

HOW TO WEAR JACKETS

One of the great versatilities of suit-jacket dressing is creating your own idea of a "suit" by putting together, for example, a black gabardine evening jacket with a long gray skirt and cream-

colored silk blouse. Or a red-and-black plaid fifties jacket that works with a black pleated skirt.

Another great way to wear an antique suit jacket: over a printed silk or rayon forties dress. If the dress has a lapel and collar, they can be worn over the jacket collar. Add a solid-colored leather belt to the printed dress (the belt color could match the jacket) and voilà, "l'ensemble." Another option, once you have tried wearing the jacket open over the dress, is closed and belted on the outside. This works well if neither the jacket nor the dress is too bulky. For a daytime jacket, expect to pay between $25 and $75, depending on detail, condition, fabric, trim.

Mexican Jackets

A favorite jacket of mine is the hand-embroidered Mexican wool "folk art" jacket from the forties and fifties. Tourists visiting Mexico brought them back as souvenirs, and some can now be found on the vintage-clothing market. (These jackets are still being made today; but the fabrics and embroidery are not the same quality.) The backs of Mexican jackets are usually embroidered with a landscape, cactus, a horse and rider, or a pair of Mexican dancers. The woman's hair is braided wool. And they come in beautiful colors—black, white, red, green, turquoise, or blue, with multicolor embroidery and appliqué.

The best places to look for these jackets are in southern California antique-clothing shops and also at the Rose Bowl flea market in Pasadena. Mexican jackets can be found in other areas of the country, too, but there are lots more to choose from on the West Coast.

Protect your wool Mexican jacket in the summer season with mothballs. Blue wool jackets often fade, especially near the shoulder and along the arm. Watch for this when choosing one.

Mexican jackets are colorful, wearable, unique. They work well with jeans and other casual pants or as spring "toppers" with a sweater or cowboy shirt underneath. Sleek black leather pants go well with the red Mexican jackets. Pam Leon wears hers with narrow cord pants and a crisp white cotton shirt on page 129.

Expect to pay between $35 and $75, depending on condition, style of embroidery, and color.

Opposite left: *An early–1940s navy gabardine jacket with padded shoulders and slightly fitted cuffs, belted with a brass-studded suede belt. Whether dress lengths are long or short, a jacket like this looks great over a print. High-heeled pumps add to the elegance.*

Above and lower right: *Multicolored appliqué, embroidery, and sequins adorn this red wool Mexican jacket. Pam Leon likes to wear hers over a white cotton shirt with narrow cord pants and a decorative leather belt.*

Below: *Ed Netherton displays one of his finds: a three-quarter-length black satin Chinese jacket, hand embroidered in gold, silver, and multicolored threads. The cuffs are embroidered bands of white satin. The jacket was probably made in the 1920s. Heavily decorated jackets always look best with simple black pants.*

Right: *A rear view of a reversible gray-and-black satin baseball-style Japanese jacket, with a multicolored scene embroidered on the outside and a tiger (unseen) on the inside. Truusje Kushner wears it over tan wool men's pants and cowboy boots.*

Oriental Jackets

Looking at fabrics from Japan and detailed Chinese embroidery could keep me busy for weeks. The Japanese printed silk fabrics that I love can be found in old kimonos. And the most beautiful Chinese embroidery is done on mandarin jackets and coats. More modern Oriental design can be found on the embroidered rayon-satin baseball jackets with fitted, ribbed waists and slash pockets, brought back from Japan after World War II and from Korea after the Korean war. The backs of these jackets were embroidered with maps of Japan and Korea, tigers, palm trees, or the names of cities. Often they were reversible, mostly blue and yellow or blue and white on one side with black on the other side. You can see an example on page 131.

Both men and women can wear the Japanese- or Korean-style baseball jacket with jeans or pleated pants. The jacket also goes well with military-style khaki twill pants, which are easy to find and wear with all jacket styles. Authentic twills, new or used, are sold in army-navy stores all over the country, and are being copied by many of today's designers.

The other interesting and wearable type of Oriental jacket is the embroidered mandarin jacket. Newer versions in rayon brocade or satin can be bought in almost any Chinatown throughout the country. Earlier versions from the nineteenth and early twentieth centuries were made of brocaded blue, black, white, salmon, or red silk satins and decorated with colorful and intricate embroidery. The embroidery, coloring, and detail are finer and more varied on older jackets. Those made after 1940 are less unusual. The best way to wear an elaborately embroidered mandarin jacket is with simple straight-leg black silk pants.

Among the best I have seen: a very fine lady's silk-lined jacket of navy satin made in the twenties, elaborately embroidered in multicolored silk threads with blue butterflies, blossoms, and large pink peonies in the "forbidden stitch," a crewel embroidery stitch used only on imperial royal family clothing. The wide sleeves had turned-back cuffs lined in saffron-yellow silk and similarly embroidered. Another example: An early thirties jacket of black satin, lined in silk and elegantly embroidered in multicolored silks with Fu dogs, butterflies, birds, goldfish, and flowering foliage, trimmed with bands of embroidered blue silk; the straight, wide sleeves were lined with embroidered white satin cuffs.

CONDITION AND CARE

Everyone who brought back Oriental baseball jackets from overseas wore them, so finding one in mint condition is nearly impossible. The jacket may often be stained. The ribbed cotton cuffs and waistband may be torn or stretched. Some embroidery may be missing. And if the jacket was washed instead of dry-cleaned, the embroidery threads may have run into the satin because they are not colorfast.

Most of the stains can be removed by a good dry cleaner, and the ribbed cotton cuffs and waist-

Left: *A classic brown leather zip-front flight jacket: brown shearling collar and front, white shearling lining, matching leather belt. Worn here over a gabardine shirt and jeans—a timeless combination.*

Right: *Ron Lieberman's favorite gabardine jacket: a fleck-patterned navy blue, reversible to pink, worn over a pink gabardine shirt with a skinny black tie. Pleated wool pants, jeans, or khaki twills would add variety to this look.*

band can be replaced by a seamstress. You can even have missing parts of the embroidered design redone. But if the colors have run, I advise you to skip purchasing the jacket. Be sure to sew up inside and outside seams that sometimes pull apart after cleaning. These jackets are so desirable that customers often buy them despite their condition. Prices are high, so I advise buying a jacket in good condition. For mint- and good-condition, reversible, embroidered jackets, expect to pay around $120.

Satin and silk Chinese mandarin jackets should be examined carefully for torn linings, faded color, dark stains around the neck, stained underarms, and missing borders. These jackets have to be dry-cleaned by a good cleaner because special care must be taken when pressing embroidery. Because these jackets are worn for dressy occasions, I don't advise purchasing those in poor condition—unless you want to use the embroidered border on another piece of clothing. If the price is cheap enough, pieces of the jacket can be used and applied on a plain silk jacket.

If you find an elaborately embroidered Chinese mandarin jacket at an auction (where they are frequently sold) and in good condition (which means you should be prepared to replace the lining, mend the border in several places, and have it dry-cleaned), it will cost between $150 and $350.

A more ordinary jacket of silk brocade with very little embroidery may sell at auction for $75 to $100.

Men's Leather Jackets

Leather has become very popular in the new-clothing market. The old-leather market is also booming, with black leather motorcycle jackets and brown leather flight jackets leading the way. The multizippered black cycle jacket, originally made of horsehide, is made today with different leathers; but they cannot compete with the quilt- or wool-lined horsehide jackets made through the fifties for police and other cyclists. The brown leather zip-front flight jackets made for Air Force men during World War II were often lined in shearling.

Look for brown leather flight jackets and black motorcycle jackets in good condition. If the front zipper on either style does not work, you can have it replaced. Most good dry cleaners can send them out for repair at a cost to you of about $25. A good leather cleaner can restore the horsehide or leather by using special creams, saddle soap, or mink oil. Wool and quilted linings can be replaced; but consider the price of the jacket together with the cost of replacing the lining before making your purchase.

A good-condition black leather motorcycle jacket with all zippers in working order and lining intact will cost about $250. A brown leather flight jacket with shearling collar or lining in good condition runs from $200 to $250.

Reversible Baseball-Style Jackets

Another classic jacket for men is the gabardine, velour, or wool reversible baseball-style jacket with ribbed wool or cotton cuffs and waistbands and slash pockets. These jackets were made in small, medium, and large in fabric and color combinations like solid-brown gabardine reversing to brown-printed gab or gold-patterned black velour lined in black satin—as seen on Raymond Jurado, page 135. Sometimes one side can be a tweedy wool; the reverse side, gray or black gabardine. Another possibility: a blue or black gab jacket, lined in navy, with a white or contrasting colored yoke, which may also be printed with a snowflake or skier motif. Or black with a white fringed yoke and pearlized snap closings to create a cowboy look.

Baseball jackets can be worn by both men and women. Large sizes are most often bought by men; women buy the smalls and some mediums. They can be worn with jeans, pleated pants, khaki pants, or colored painter's pants. A button-down oxford-cloth shirt can be worn underneath, as well as a T-shirt or gabardine shirt. A scarf at the neck in plaid cashmere or Deco silk is a good accessory.

Prices, depending on condition, color, reversibility, and fabrics, range from $40 to $80.

Tweeds

Forties and fifties men's wool tweed jackets with two or three buttons have been selling to vintage-clothing connoisseurs for years. They're colorful and wearable and come in tweedy mixtures of black, white, and gray; gray, white, blue, and red; brown, gold, rust, and white; blue, gray, red, and cream. Almost any combination is possible. Searching for a unique tweed is like searching for any other fashion treasure: It takes time, but the results—and the price (lower than new versions)—make the search worthwhile. Two labels to look for: Bond's and Penney's—they made a lot of colorful tweed jackets, as well as black-and-white tweedy ones.

Men wear tweed jackets with jeans, gabardine, or flannel pleated pants, cord pants, cotton twills, or "unmatched" tweed pants. Women mix them with printed silk skirts and blouses, khaki pants and oxford shirts, or jeans and gabardine shirts. A boy's or man's tweed jacket is a fun addition to a woman's wardrobe and can be mixed and matched with almost everything you own, just like a suit jacket.

Because of the nubby surface of tweed fabrics, it is harder to find damage spots, such as stains and moth holes. If a tweed jacket is unlined (most of these sports jackets are), hold it up to the light to examine it more carefully. Look for missing buttons and sleeves that have been shortened too much.

Tweed sports jackets in boy's sizes 16, 18, 20 (good for many women) cost around $45 to $50. Men's sizes (36–44) run from $45 to $65.

Left: *Designer Raymond Jurado pairs this gold-patterned black velour jacket lined in black satin with a black T-shirt, gabardine shirt, jeans, and leather belt.*

Below: *A 1950s tweed jacket makes a durable, contemporary, and easy-to-wear outfit with jeans or wool trousers and any sort of striped cotton or gabardine shirt.*

15

Furs: Economical Recycling

Articles in women's magazines sometimes advise women not to buy old furs because of their condition. Fur is very perishable; more so when it is not stored or cared for properly. But if you buy vintage fur carefully, you can come out ahead—both in appeal and price. After all, never have new furs been more expensive, and prices are getting higher all the time. Going vintage is a good alternative.

How often should you replace or add a fur? That depends . . . on your fickleness, for one thing, and on how tired you get of your coat's style. Fashion, too, plays a part. Hems go up or come down, sometimes just after you've altered your fur. One year the look is big and furry; the next it's slim and flat. No working woman can afford to buy a new fur every other year. And you shouldn't have to. A good rule of thumb is one new fur about every ten years if your budget permits, and one or two vintage furs to supplement that, for variety.

Before we even discuss the differences among furs and styles, there are a few important rules you should know about. It takes a good fur shopper to buy for style and good condition.

- Furs that have not been stored properly dry out and skins split apart. Certain spots should be checked carefully before buying. Always feel under the arms and around the shoulders; check elbows and pockets for rips. Look for bald areas along the front closing and the cuffs.
- Long-hair furs are harder to check but easier to repair. You can't see splits as easily, but you can't see repairs after they are done either.
- Ask the seller if he or she knows whether any repairs have been done in the fur you are considering—especially if it is a long-hair fur, because you can't see repairs as easily as you can in a short-hair fur. And if the shoulder, for instance, has been repaired several times,

you want to know that, because you may not want to buy.

· Touch the underside of the fur under the lining. It should feel supple and should not make a crackling sound when squeezed between your fingers. Do *not* buy furs that are dry and brittle to the touch.

If all of these things check out, the next questions to ask are the following: How old is the coat? and How much is it? Price should relate—reasonably—to the fur's condition. For example, if you spot an early fifties mouton coat (a heavy, warm "knock-around" fur for casual wear) at a yard sale, and it has a clean, untorn lining—you have a bargain at $150.

What about a twenty-five-year-old restyled mink jacket, with a new lining, no rips or tears. If the mink has a good sheen and hasn't oxidized (turned reddish), it is going to be a good buy at $450. If you are lucky enough to find one of the fifties seven-eighths-length coats with a full-swing back, you may have enough fur to restyle it into a full-length slim mink coat. Since prices of brand-new ranch mink coats are high (and "wild mink" is even higher), vintage mink can be a bargain. But don't be hasty; even the best furrier in town can't bring back the original rich dark color to a mink if it has oxidized.

Fox

If you find a silver fox chubby jacket with its fur in good condition (no worn, matted spots or bald cuffs) and the lining is clean and intact, expect to pay about $750 and up. Keep in mind that old fox is very perishable, and if it was not stored properly it will not last. Chances are that the fox you are buying is about forty years old; silver fox chubby jackets were designed in the forties. If the condition is good it will probably last you another three to five seasons. Fox chubbies, also made in white, red, and platina (a white and beige coloring), are glamorous "movie star" furs, best saved for special nights out for the glamour-minded shopper, who should have another basic fur coat at home for everyday wear. If you want fox, you're wise to go for boas and stoles, which wear much better than coats; I have few customer complaints about how these hold up.

Mole, Monkey, Muskrat

Mole is a soft, flat, gray fur that does not wear long or well because it is "porous." Mole, along with mink and ermine, was used to trim wool or lamé coats along the collar and cuffs, or to cover buttons in the twenties; by the thirties, mole jackets and coats had become stylish. Coat cuffs and front edges trimmed in mole are prone to baldness, and mole fur will dry out and tear after a while.

Monkey comes in black, black and white, or, in rare cases, all white. It was usually made into short chubby jackets and coats in the thirties and forties. Monkey is another porous fur that wears easily at the neck and can dry out and split at the shoulder. Tears in the sleeves and under the arms are also common; look for these.

In spite of its shortcomings, monkey is much in demand. One customer of mine, a lyricist who

Left: Mouton, *a sheared lamb, was made in the forties and fifties in brown and honey tones and styled with padded shoulders, swing back, and turned-up cuffs. It was considered a poor-girl's seal and is sometimes mistaken for seal today. Alexandra Penney bought hers for fun and warmth at a bargain price and commissioned Jack Goldman to add expensive, intricate designs of copper and gold beads and jewels to the collar and cuffs, turning her everyday mouton into a widely admired fashion item.*

Bottom left: *Mink, the pelt of a small brown weasel bred mostly in the United States, is coveted throughout the world for its sheen, durability, warmth, and light weight. Vintage mink such as this 1950s three-quarter-length jacket is hard to come by and expensive; this one shows a cut often found in various furs of the fifties: a wrap style with wide sleeve and turned cuff.*

Bottom right: *A short black monkey jacket with padded shoulders and black crocheted collar and cuffs, worn over gray cashmere slacks. It is best for special occasions over silk or wool trousers or soft crepe dresses.*

had occasion to go to rock concerts and parties, bought a monkey coat after all the warnings I gave her. "I don't care if it falls apart on my back," she said. "I'm wearing it for as long as I can—I have to have it." Ingrid Bergman once came into my store and headed straight for a monkey coat I had on display, saying: "This must be my coat; it looks exactly like one I owned in the forties!"

If you own a monkey coat or jacket and want to keep it awhile, wear it infrequently—and stay out of the rain.

Muskrat, on the other hand, was the "poor woman's mink" in the thirties and forties. Muskrats were often dyed to look like mink, and many people today buy vintage muskrat thinking they have a wild mink coat (which in today's mink market is rare and expensive). But when muskrat—a brownish-gray fur—falls apart, it really goes to pieces. Many vintage-clothing dealers can easily find muskrats, so there are a lot of coats and jackets for sale. More often than not they are poorly repaired. Buy muskrat only when it is very inexpensive or looks and feels almost new. You can pick up a muskrat coat or jacket for $45 at a flea market; it may get you through a winter season, but even if it falls apart, it's kept you warmer than any cloth coat you could buy. So before you buy, evaluate: price, condition, how long you want your fur to last.

Padded-Shoulder Furs: Persian and Karakul Lamb, Pony, Raccoon

Persian and karakul lamb, pony, and raccoon are three other vintage furs that have become fashionable again. A few years ago women gave away their black or gray Persians; they were so heavy and unfashionable, and everyone wanted mink. Now Persian lamb is back in fashion and is being used again by well-known contemporary designers. I find lamb an ideal fur. If you find one in good condition, you have a coat worth restyling. Look for the simple padded-shoulder styles of the forties or the full swing-backs of the fifties; you may not want to restyle either of these. The only drawback is its weight—Persian lamb skins are heavy, although the skins are lighter in coats made today. Longer-haired karakul is also lighter weight.

Pony coats were common in the twenties and thirties, so when you find one, keep in mind how old it must be. If it has padded shoulders and big sleeves, it's probably from the forties and hence in better condition. Pony is a flat fur and comes in black, white, or spotted brown and white. The coat should not feel stiff to the touch; if it does, it is dried out.

Everyone who has thought of vintage fur naturally thinks of the long, shawl-collared raccoon coats worn by college boys in the twenties. The styling of women's raccoon coats from that period was very similar. As we move into the thirties, forties, and fifties, styling became a little looser, and these more recent furs should feel more supple. (Twenties raccoons feel too stiff to me; I never buy them for my shop.) The padded-shoulder, wide-sleeved, three-quarter-length raccoons from the thirties, forties, and fifties are the most appealing. Often the pelts were worked on the diagonal, creating a chevron pattern. Vintage raccoons in this style have gone up in price in the last few years because they wear well. In good condition, vintage raccoon costs about $600. If you find one, you can feel confident that you've made a good buy.

Rabbit and Seal

Seal and rabbit resemble each other when they are dyed black. *Lapin*, as rabbit is called by French and American furriers, was the poor woman's seal. In the thirties and forties, so many rabbit coats were made that, besides muskrat, I don't know of any other fur as available. However, rabbit doesn't wear well. Rabbit is porous, and when it is old and dry it rips easily. The most interesting use of rabbit in the forties and fifties was the stenciled pattern of leopard and cheetah that often fools today's vintage fur buyer. From a distance a stenciled rabbit coat could resemble a leopard. But look deep into the fur past the surface, and voilà, rabbit.

Seal is a more desirable fur and makes a good (warm!) everyday solution to cold weather. One seal I recently sold had padded shoulders, large puffed sleeves, a full back, and no collar. Keiko Miyasaka, who bought it, tied the bright blue leather belt she had worn into the shop around

Above: *Photographer Gustavo Candelas nearly froze to death snapping this photo of two models hailing a taxi in eleven-degree weather. On the left is a 1940s gray Russian lamb, knee length, worn with very high dark gray boots: and on the right is a 1950s honey-colored mink-dyed musk-rat with pronounced stripes, worn with wool ski pants and boots.*

Left: *Gina looks stylish and warm in a forties gray rabbit coat of seven-eighths length, worn over a forties print dress and accented with a cut-velvet fringed scarf. The coat has padded shoulders—typical of the forties—and its lining is a lovely gray silk.*

Above: *Ermine was once worn only by royalty, and in the twenties and thirties it was still a symbol of wealth. Good vintage ermine is hard to find because the fur doesn't hold up well. White rabbit as a trim on coats and jackets is often mistaken for ermine. Peggy's thirties ermine jacket is worn belted with black tuxedo trousers.*

Right: *A rich brown knee-length seal coat with padded shoulders and fitted cuffs. Keiko belts it with bright blue leather and wears it with high boots to make a very contemporary look.*

the waist—and left wearing the coat, looking great. (See photograph on page 142.)

Boas: Heads and Tails

Many of our mothers had shoulder and neck pieces of fox, mink, stone marten, or sable. Each boa was made from a small animal with the head (complete with glass eyes), body, feet, and tails. Usually two or three skins made up a boa, but some had as many as six. A very pretty and practical way of wearing a boa is as a fur muffler rather than as a shoulder piece. To do this, take the pelts apart and have the animals resewn head to tail in a straight line rather than side to side, as they originally came. And instead of tying it, add a hook and eye on two of the feet to keep the boa around your neck. I own a ranch-mink boa altered like this, and I wear it often—it's not too dressy—over sweaters or a sporty tweed coat. Phyllis Newman wears a long silver fox boa she recently bought from my shop with dressy gowns or over a black wool coat.

A Few Words About Endangered Spotted Cats

From the thirties through the fifties, ocelot, leopard, and cheetah were frequently made into luxurious coats. Magazine photographs of society women from this period show lots of full-length leopard coats, with matching hats and muffs.

In 1973 the United States Congress passed the Endangered Species Act to protect certain fish and wildlife from extinction. Among the animals included are ocelot, leopard, cheetah, alligator, crocodile, and turtle. (Alligator has recently been exempted, because American alligators are now overpopulated.) The law says you cannot import or sell (even from your home) any protected wildlife for personal or commercial use. This includes any product made from this wildlife after 1830. Although some tortoise combs and dressing-table accessories made from turtle shell may be from the pre-1830 period, most tortoise items you see for sale were made after 1900—and are really being sold illegally. Other "tortoise" items are not the real thing but are actually made of Bakelite or Celluloid—among the earliest plastics.

This means, of course, that you cannot buy a coat made of any of these furs. If you have inherited a rare spotted-cat fur, and you happen to wear it on a trip out of the country, you must be able to prove that it belonged to you before you left or it will be confiscated by U.S. Customs on your return. The best way to do this is to have the coat stamped (on the inside of the fur) by the customs department before leaving the country.

Home Repairs and Care

If you own a vintage fur, it's a good idea to have on hand fur tape, fur thread, and a special triangular fur needle for easy home repairs. You can get these and other supplies at the large and famous store Samuel Bauer & Sons, 145 West 29th Street, New York, New York 10001, 212-868-4190; they fill orders from out of town.

To sew up splits: Open the lining near the split; sew up the rip on the suede side, using an overhand stitch. Next, cut the fur tape to fit the shape and the length of the tear. Place the tape (fabric on one side; "gummy" on the other) generously over the area, pressing and smoothing it over the tear. *Never* iron the tape. Resew the lining.

For cleaning and repairing old furs, check out:

Aronowicz Furs
345 Seventh Avenue
New York, New York 10001
212-695-1485

Germaine Furs
330 Seventh Avenue
New York, New York 10001
212-695-0645

Harry Kirshner & Son
307 Seventh Avenue
New York, New York 10001
212-243-4847

16

Scarves: To Own by the Dozens

Many vintage-clothes buyers began their collecting with the purchase of a scarf or a vintage fringed muffler. Then they were hooked forever on the enormous variety of antique clothing available.

My own scarf collection numbers fifty, which I keep in a vanity drawer. Most of them are so beautiful that I take them out to admire them more often than I wear them. I feel as though I own fifty paintings, all hidden away. Some resemble little beaded necklaces. One kerchief I found in California is trimmed with seashells. Another is a pocket square in the shape of a large bunch of flowers; it looks just like a flower in your pocket when it's worn.

Men's Fringed Scarves

If you have seen antique scarves at flea markets or vintage-clothing boutiques, you've probably noticed the fringed oblong scarves that women and men have been wearing with everything for years. The most widely available ones come in rayon or silk. Designs can be paisley, geometric, or Art Deco; jacquards, polka dots, and foulards of many kinds. The patterns are endless—but the colorings are somewhat limited. It is harder to find blacks and reds now, though navy, burgundy, and brown are plentiful. Harder to find: a green silk scarf with an abstract Deco design. Ditto, a cream-colored fine silk one with fresh-looking silk fringe, and perhaps an initial. A. Sulka and Company made some of the most desirable silk scarves—long and wide, in heavy silks, with rich colorations and simple but elegant patterns. Another label to look for: the Cisco Company, which made some of the funkiest and most Deco-looking scarves in heavy rayon fabrics, with strong colorations or contrasts.

Other fun jacquard designs include figuratives: cowboy, skiing, fisherman, or horsey patterns; in

Top: *Three 1940s men's fringed scarves: (left) a burgundy rayon jacquard with a Deco geometric print; (center) a uniquely patterned scarf in silk, beige design on brown and brown design on beige, with beige-and-brown fringe; (right) a deep royal blue jacquard with burgundy, blue, and beige design and all three colors in the silk fringe.*

Left: *A wine, cream, and black patterned jacquard goes well draped over the shoulders of a salt-and-pepper tweed 1950s coat.*

navy, burgundy, yellow, or off-white colorings. These make great gifts for horsemen and sports lovers. Look for unusual colors and patterns that you have not seen anywhere. Try to keep away from anything synthetic.

A few guidelines: When buying a scarf, always check that the fringe doesn't look as frizzy as a forties home hair permanent. The creased edges of fine silk scarves sometimes split, so be careful; you can't see splits easily because of this crease. Old rust or oil stains on white scarves usually will not come off.

For cold winter days, try to find pure silk scarves with cashmere liners, which can be worn on either side to make two scarves in one. But don't make the mistake of thinking that these scarves can be washed easily because one side is wool; they can't. One of my customers tried; the cashmere liner shrank and the silk side ran.

Silkscreened Printed Scarves

The favorite scarves of collectors are the large, multicolored, hand-blocked or screen-printed silk square or oblong. I have one that depicts a Nantucket water scene—with pink clouds floating on an aqua sky and a brown bridge dotted with fishermen. Another I framed: a perfect purple orchid with a yellow center and green leaves. It is often mistaken for a painting; once I was offered $500 for it! The subject of hand-printed scarves can vary widely—everything from a face to a simple, two-color geometric design. The way to recognize a silkscreened printed scarf is to look at the edges of the pattern; hand-screened prints are rarely perfect. Look at the pattern on the fabric; the color will be slightly out of register, not perfectly printed like a mass-produced design.

Collecting Small Squares

Neckerchiefs and other small squares that were made for school kids or as souvenirs are very collectible and wearable as pocket handkerchiefs. The subject matter of these scarves could fill a book: *Gone With the Wind* had a scarf made in its honor, with all the *GWTW* characters colorfully printed on silk, as did *The Wizard of Oz*. Many small squares were printed in commemora-

tion of the 1939 World's Fair; and hundreds of collectors of World's Fair memorabilia covet them.

In my collection are small squares depicting cigarettes; well-known cowboys of the past, riding their broncos; Atlantic City and its boardwalk; Tillie the Toiler, from the 1920s comic strip; an exercise scene showing women getting their bodies in shape; a horoscope from the 1930s; scenes of the landing of the pilgrims and the discovery of America.

Special Scarves

Hermès silk scarves from the forties, fifties, and sixties are not inexpensive collectibles; but they certainly are less expensive than the new ones sold here and in Paris. For many women, the Hermès squares are elegant and carry status. They come in a wide range of patterns: florals, horse themes, mushrooms, architecture, and so on. Copies of Hermès scarves were made in the sixties, so look for the name *Hermès* on any Hermès scarf you seek. Some people can still find them inexpensively in thrift shops; the last one I had sold for $35.

Some of the more expensive scarf collectibles are multicolor embroidered or silkscreened shawls with hand-tied fringe. When I first went into business, every flea market and antique show showed at least four or five of these shawls—and at very reasonable prices. Shawls with Chinese motifs—embroidered birds, flowers, Oriental people, and Chinese ideograms—were often as little as $40. The fringe was full and the colors never faded. The most popular motif of these shawls: large red cabbage roses scattered against a black silk ground—called Spanish shawls, because flamenco dancers wore them. The most beautiful embroidered shawls I've ever bought for my shop are Chinese, with subtly embroidered colored designs and hand-knotted silk fringe, made in the nineteenth and early twentieth centuries. The handwork is so fine that you can't tell the wrong side from the right side—except for the small knots tying off the embroidery.

Printed shawls from the twenties and thirties have pastel-colored Art Deco designs in silkscreened hues of coral, turquoise, fuchsia, apricot, rose, gray, and blue—all "swirled" together in deli-

Two amusing large square silkscreened scarves of the fifties, both one of a kind: (opposite top right) *a menu in royal blue and white, with multicolored food design;* (opposite bottom left) *an advertisement scarf on cream silk colored in everything from fuchsia and black to turquoise and yellow. Two designs in the endless array of small rayon squares:* (opposite top left) *an exercise motif in red, black, yellow, and white;* (opposite bottom right) *and a 1939 World's Fair scarf in red, white, and blue.*

Below left: *A very large black net 1920s Egyptian silver shawl from my collection. The amount of silver design makes this a coveted item. It looks beautiful around the collar of a black cashmere coat; sometimes I drape it over one shoulder and pin it at the waist over a black cashmere sweater and pants.* Below right: *The versatile, collectible shawl: this one with lots of hand-knotting and fringe, in mauve-colored chiffon and cocoa, aqua, pink, and gold flocked velvet. Worn here as a cover-up for a sheer camisole.*

How to wear scarves: (above) Nina Malkin ties a long lace scarf into a bow at the neck of a simple wool sweater; (below) Nina drapes this sequined silk-chiffon square around the shoulders and tucks it into a leather belt; (opposite) Marilis Flusser wears a silk Hermès scarf around her head and knots it in the back.

ica by tourists, they were usually referred to as Egyptian silver shawls. The flattened hand-placed staples are not of sterling silver but silver over copper, and the gold-toned staples are brass. Brass and silver sometimes tarnish in spots, but this should not stop you from purchasing an Egyptian shawl. Shawls made of white netting can be bleached if they turn yellowish. They can also easily be dyed in very hot water.

By the way, scarves make great gifts for men and women, especially at Christmastime. One holiday season I devoted an entire window to scarves in every style and color. As each scarf in the display was sold, I replaced it with another one, equally beautiful. The display had great appeal, and my customers thought my scarf supply was endless! Actress Linda Lavin came into the store and bought five men's fringed Art Deco scarves. By the last two days before Christmas, I had fewer than fifteen left, and they were all gone by Christmas Eve.

How to Wear Scarves

Wear scarves over coats and blazers, tucked into V-neck sweaters, wrapping the waist as a belt, or around the shoulders for warmth and style. A large shawl can also be tied at the waist and worn as a skirt. Or use the shawls as throws—as a unique bedspread or a piano cover. An oblong silk scarf tied around the bosom makes a great halter. Invent your own way to twist and tie a small square scarf at the neck.

Prices

Here's the range you can expect to pay for scarves.

Men's fringed scarves: $10–$40
Silkscreened printed scarves: $25–$100
Small square scarves: $10–$25
Hand-embroidered silk shawls with fringe: $100–$650
Egyptian silver shawls: $65–$350

cate abstract patterns. They are very collectible; the printed shawls I've had in my shop have always been snapped up by designers, decorators, and art collectors.

Egyptian silver shawls were made in the twenties and thirties of handwoven black or white linen in an open-net weave, with hand-applied silver- or gold-toned "staples" placed in geometric designs over the netting. Designs included rows of stick-figure trees, camels, houses, and people. Other designs are done in diamond shapes, placed in sections across the long, narrow shawl, which measures two feet by six feet. Although these shawls were made in Morocco, India, and Egypt and were brought back to England and Amer-

17

Accessories: More Mileage for Your Money

If you shop the vintage-clothing stores, you know that shoes, belts, hats, and purses are easy to find in good condition and are moderately priced. Not only are accessories easy to buy for yourself, but they make great gifts—especially when you don't know a friend's size.

In most boutiques you can count on finding every type of accessory from elegant and expensive to funky but usable things that sell for only a few dollars. I have always collected both for myself and keep the same mixture in my shop. One day I may wear a 1920s gold Cartier bracelet and a gold-kid belt; the next day, I may switch to wearing ten plastic bangle bracelets with a Lucite belt. You can collect different types of accessories within a single wardrobe—you don't have to stick to one accessory style. And if you pull it together right, different types of accessories can even be mixed together in one outfit.

One of the most rewarding aspects of accessory collecting is that you don't have to feel guilty about spending heaps of money on it. When customers buy a dress, coat, or silk blouse, they often feel terrible about spending a lot of money. It is a delight to buy small things—and a lot of them, at reasonable prices. When I buy shoes, purses, or belts for the shop, I am more excited than when I buy clothes. There is a special surprise or sense of discovery in making small purchases that I sometimes don't experience when buying clothes. My dressing table at home is covered with purses, jewelry, belts, and beads, all of which hang around my mirror so that I can see the full range of what I have to choose from when I'm dressing.

Shoes

If you are a collector and happen to own a pair of Victorian satin wedding slippers or white kid boots, pass them on to your daughter or niece. They will never fit the foot of an adult woman,

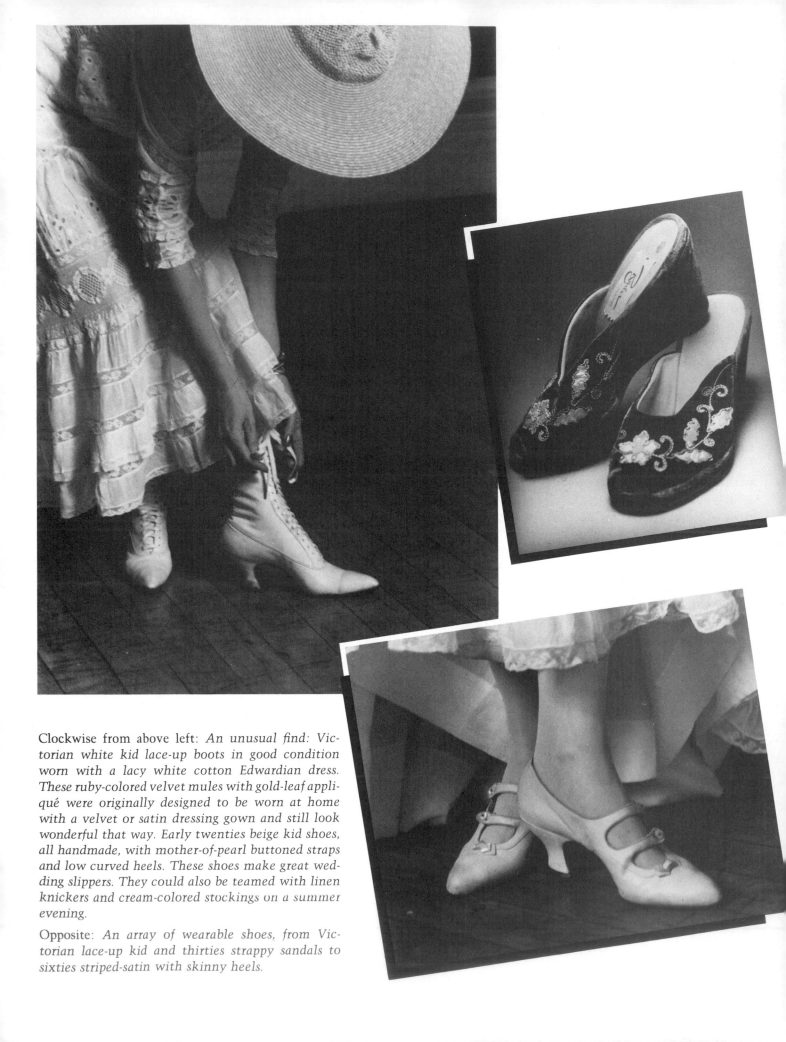

Clockwise from above left: *An unusual find: Vic-torian white kid lace-up boots in good condition worn with a lacy white cotton Edwardian dress. These ruby-colored velvet mules with gold-leaf appli-qué were originally designed to be worn at home with a velvet or satin dressing gown and still look wonderful that way. Early twenties beige kid shoes, all handmade, with mother-of-pearl buttoned straps and low curved heels. These shoes make great wed-ding slippers. They could also be teamed with linen knickers and cream-colored stockings on a summer evening.*

Opposite: *An array of wearable shoes, from Vic-torian lace-up kid and thirties strappy sandals to sixties striped-satin with skinny heels.*

but they will fit hers. Victorian daytime leather shoes are so small and narrow that today's store owners use them for display purposes, with the hope that a tiny-footed woman may appear in the shop one day and purchase them. When you find a pair of Victorian shoes you want that fit, have them fixed so you can wear them in the street. (Old unrefurbished leather can't tolerate city streets or any hard surfaces.) Always have new soles, heels, and taps put on.

My two favorite decades for shoe design are the twenties and thirties. Twenties styles (most of which were handmade) included T-straps, beaded buckle fronts, low hourglass heels. Materials were soft, fine leathers in custom colors such as chocolate brown and silver kid and silk with mother-of-pearl or rhinestone button instep closings. Thirties shoes had slightly higher, straighter heels, usually open toes, instep and T-strap buckle closings, and were made of fine leathers and colorful suedes and leathers for day wear. Evening shoes were made in fine gold and silver leathers and brocade and richly colored velvets. (See photograph of a pair of ruby velvet thirties mules on page 154.)

Today it is nearly impossible to find a hand-made shoe—costs are prohibitive. Leather prices go up every year by at least 20 percent. If you find a pair of dress shoes from either of these two decades that's in good condition, you're in luck. Always check the leather for dryness and stiffness. If there are straps and buckles, make sure they are in wearable condition. If not, have a shoemaker replace them. Don't buy vintage shoes if they are cracking or peeling around the toe or if they don't fit. Looking for proper fit in vintage shoes is no different from looking for fit in a new pair. Don't buy them if they don't fit properly. Lots of twenties and thirties shoes were narrow and small.

Satin bedroom shoes were favorite Christmas gifts in the forties and fifties. They were originally meant to be worn as house slippers, but the low chunky heel makes them ideal today as a dancing slipper or evening shoe. I find them in pink, black, or burgundy; some have marabou trim. Look for these; they are very comfortable to wear and cheaper than evening shoes.

The best of all possible worlds is finding shoes that have never been worn. They could be from stock that was never sold in a shoe store. Or they

A selection of vintage purses: (clockwise from upper left.) a black, blue, and gray 1920s Deco leather clutch; a multicolored 1940s clutch made up of plastic sections connected with plastic thread; a purse I made from a sterling Victorian frame and a piece of early Chinese embroidery found at a flea market; a signed 1918 Weiner Werkstatte purse of handwoven silk— valuable and collectible; two enameled metal-mesh purses from the twenties; a classic white metal Whiting & Davis purse from the thirties with white Celluloid frame and clasp and chain handle.

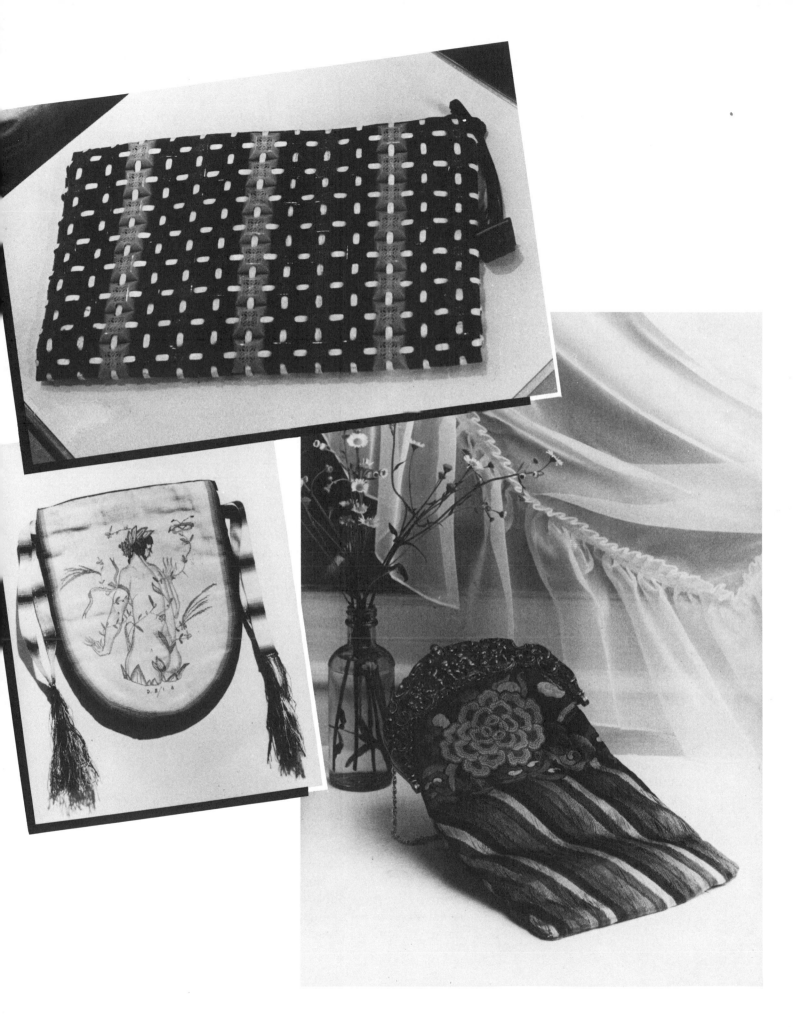

could come from a house sale where the clothing and shoes were never worn.

Men are always on the lookout for white, blue, or brown suede shoes. In my shop men's shoes sell faster than women's—mostly because men's styles don't change as much; so anything made from 1900 to the 1950s is still in fashion. Many men are especially fond of two-color shoes, such as brown and white, or black and white, in perforated leather.

Purses

I've always known a lot of shoe lovers, but lately purse lovers have come out of the closet in hordes—including myself, although I was a late bloomer. I began to love purses about twelve years ago, and now I can't stop collecting them. I own alligators, silver-and-enameled-mesh purses, and, of course, beaded ones, too. A special prize: a vintage lizard clutch from Lederer that half the New York fashion world covets; when I take it to a nightclub, it never leaves my lap.

When you shop for a purse, you'll be able to find a vast collection of fabrics, embroideries, brocades, beads, and leathers. I recently bought a purse collection that included Victorian beaded wallets, petit point boxes and pouches with sterling silver and marcasite frames, gold and satin brocades, black silks with Art Deco clasps, gold-trimmed snakeskin, a red leather one with a mirror, comb, and tiny ivory fan inside. Customers bought these purses as little treasures.

When looking for a purse for frequent use, try to find one in nearly new condition. Old leather can be dry and stiff and may peel. Softness in leather is the key. If you pick up a Victorian beaded bag in a shop and beads clatter to the floor, leave it behind or be prepared to invest in a beading needle, and lots of time, to repair it.

Because evening purses are seldom used, they can usually be found in excellent condition. Linings are clean, and there's often an old lacy hanky, with a faint smell of perfume, still tucked inside.

If you like metals, consider silver, gold, or enameled mesh. A purse marked "German silver" (look on the inside of the frame) is not silver at all but made mostly of nickel. A "name" to look

for: Whiting and Davis, who made finely designed metal-mesh purses in the twenties with colorful Art Deco motifs. Often the enamel came off if the purse was used frequently. I was once lucky enough to find some that were never used and were still sitting in their original boxes.

Beaded box purses from the forties have been attracting purse fanatics for the past few years. Not only do buyers love the beading and fake tortoiseshell, but they love the boxy shape. The beading on these purses was done by hand in iridescent bronze, blue, black, and silver, which was then placed over a round, square, or oval box and lined. A mirror was added to the inside cover. Carrying around a purse the size of a lunch pail doesn't strike me as particularly functional or comfortable, though it can be a conversation piece. I put a cylindrical black box bag on my coffee table from time to time as a piece of beaded art.

Silver pocketbook frames either studded with stones or decorated with carved animals are great finds. I have bought a few and made some extraordinary purses with them. If this do-it-yourself idea appeals to you, be sure the frames you buy have holes in them for attaching the fabric purse. Those frames that hold the purse by stuffing the fabric into the frame never work the second time around. Someone must have known how to years ago, but it seems impossible to accomplish now. Also be sure the hinges on the frame are in working order—so you can open and close the purse. Then create a pattern for your pouch shape, use a beaded or embroidered fabric, make a lining, and there it is—an original. I found a beautifully worked silver purse frame once and attached a strip of embroidered work from an old Chinese mandarin coat that had fallen to ruin. (See page 157 for the results.)

A change purse to challenge one's ingenuity is the Victorian "miser's purse"—a long, narrow, crocheted bag often decorated with cut-steel beads. The trick is getting into it, and that's how the purse got its name. It still makes a good secret money stash. Try hanging one from your belt.

One suggestion: Don't ever overload an old purse with too much gear. Don't stuff your life's savings, makeup, and ballet leotard into a delicate purse!

Once you own a few vintage purses, you'll get hooked. Purse collecting can become an obsession with endless choices—Victorian beading, leathers and suedes, gold or silver—from at least a hundred years of design and craftsmanship.

Belts

What changes a too-large forties silk dress into a wearable size? A belt! From Victorian silver to men's classic leathers to fifties cinch belts, the possibilities are endless. Coats can be belted to change the look—or the size. Women can belt men's silk shirts over jeans. Cowboy belts work on everything from dresses to jodhpurs. Try a vintage hand-tooled cowboy belt over a white heavy cotton Victorian nightgown.

Looking for belts is not any different from searching out vintage shoes or purses. Decide that you want a nice collection of vintage belts and look for them in every store and flea market that you visit. One of the similarities you'll find when shopping for these three accessories is that many of them are made of leather, whose condition can make or break your purchase. Stiffness or peeling, as I have mentioned before, tells you the life expectancy of the belt. Most people search out old leathers, lizards, and hand-tooled craftsmanship because newer versions are not as detailed and are much more expensive.

Hand beading was done by Native Americans on tooled leather for tourists as late as the sixties. And early Indian silver buckles are highly prized. If you happen to find an old silver buckle, you can create your own belt. The leather-and-silver combination was a favorite of English Victorians, who also made beautiful belts in nickel or sterling silver. Wearing one can completely change the look of anything you wear.

A few years ago it looked as though the wide belt of the fifties had died a "fashion death," but these are showing up on customers again. I am particularly fond of the ones that have metal emblems on the front or trinkets sewn all over them. Some curved or shaped belts from this decade are trimmed with French souvenirs. Others are nostalgically covered with pictures of jitterbuggers. One unusual belt in my collection could be considered a piece of American folk art. It is made of brown

suede and covered with handmade metal, bone, wood, and mother-of-pearl buttons. I suspect it was someone's personal project.

You can create fabric belts constantly with plain or embroidered strips of fabric, suede, or leather (about 45 inches long) and a collection of silver or enameled buckles and pins. An Art Nouveau silver buckle, for example, may lend itself to leather or fabric. Once you get the hang of putting belts together and seeing how many combinations are open to you, dressing with accessories—in an original way—will become easier and fun. But don't get discouraged: For some it is a natural knack; for others it needs developing, experimentation, and some fashion risk taking.

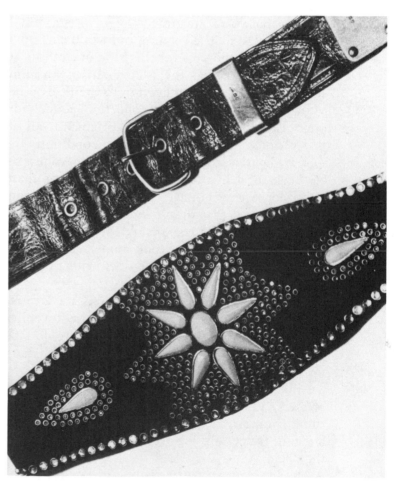

Two unusual and wearable belts: a turn-of-the-century green lizard with sterling-silver links; and a black antelope with rhinestones and turquoises studding the center in a somewhat Indian design. (Many other interesting belts are pictured with various outfits throughout the book.)

Hats

The largest and best collection of hats I ever had for sale was from a wealthy New York family. I bought the collection in 1968 from a woman whose apartment was one of the largest I'd ever seen. Everywhere I turned there were paintings by Corot, Degas, and Turner. On a beautifully polished table in the large foyer, fifty hats had been put on display for me to examine. There were 1910 velvets with plumes, twenties cloches, thirties felts with small brims—all trimmed and in immaculate condition. The owner of this palatial apartment greeted me at the door wearing terry-cloth slippers and a fifties housedress known as a "swirl."

Naturally, I bought all the hats—and some dresses, too, from 1905 to 1920. The dresses were rather ornate and costume-y for my taste, but I was fascinated by the beading and workmanship. I didn't have a following for this kind of clothing at the time, so I called the Metropolitan Museum and sold much of the collection to their Costume Institute. What made this collection perfect for the museum was the expensive, original detail of that period and the nearly unworn condition.

Straw boaters, top hats, and derbies have probably been used in more theater productions than any other type of vintage clothing. I've never seen a 1910 musical that didn't include someone singing "By the Light of the Silvery Moon" and wearing a boater. Today they look modern on women when worn with a sailor-style shirt, with a pleated skirt or shorts.

Beaver and collapsible silk top hats are surprisingly popular. Beaver is earlier and more stovepipe in shape (picture Abe Lincoln); collapsible silk hats came later and are easier to wear with tails for formal occasions.

Bankers still buy and wear derbies (also called bowlers) in London. What a sight! I happen to think women can look quite good in derbies and tails for certain big-evening occasions, such as the opera.

The big-brim straw hat is one of vintage clothing's most romantic accessories. During the late sixties and early seventies, there was a fashion for this hat, worn with a white lawn dress that had ribbons streaming from the waist. Some customers combined the big-brim hat with long thirties chiffon dresses. And many women found these hats to be the perfect touch for a wedding costume. Today they look more contemporary with white cotton pants and shirts or as beach hats.

Another great hat is the cloche—a small, tight-fitting hat that covers the head. It was the basic hat look of the twenties but has been revived enough times to be somewhat modern. The cloche hat was most frequently made of felt, with a huge variety of trims—from ribbons to buckles or feathers. It looks best when worn with a short hairstyle—so the hat becomes the central focus. A long, thin face does not lend itself well to a cloche, because it will exaggerate the length. I have found cloches in crocheted gold braid, lamé, handmade straw, satin (with a purse to match), and even covered with colorful beading. For the person who can wear a cloche, it is a great accessory with a suit or dinner outfit at night.

One of my favorites is the asymmetrical felt hat of the early forties, which fits the head closely, has no brim, and has trim that curls, twists, or stands out at one side of the head. It has a sculptured appearance and is often done in a bright color or elegant-looking black felt. Anyone who wears a hat like this instinctively feels a sense of confidence. It adds height to the wearer and presence to her appearance. But not everyone can wear this look or feel comfortable in it. Dramatic looks, well-made-up eyes, and the proper haircut help pull it off. A Dutch-boy cut or ponytail won't work.

A last word on hats: There is a special customer for them, because they are not flattering on everyone. The casual dresser who likes skirts, sweaters, and pants is not the person to be sporting a felt or feathered hat. Special occasions like theatrical openings or splashy weddings lend themselves to hat wearing. And if you can carry a hat off, nothing is more eye-catching!

Putting It All Together

Accessories add dimension and detail to a simple classic dress or tailored suit. They dress up or dress down a plain jumpsuit or silk blouse and wool skirt. They are the eye-catching details that *make* a paint-the-town-red outfit. Putting it all together with style is not the easiest job, but it

Left: *This honey-colored, wide-brim straw with grosgrain ribbon band—a typical thirties hat—adds a finishing touch to the white eyelet-and-lace Edwardian dress. Wide-brim straw hats also work well as sun protectors for beach or deck.*

Below: *A straw hat with flowers, fabric band, and net, typical of 1910–15, fun to wear with summer whites or as a fanciful touch with casual but bare clothing such as this spaghetti-strapped camisole.*

Barbara Greenwald collects hats from every era and wears them on dressy occasions. Two from the 1940s: (below) a black asymmetrical felt, and (right) a burgundy felt with a crown of bright pink grosgrain ribbon. Both are worn dramatically tilted over one eye and complement a forties fox boa.

affords plenty of opportunity to exercise your imagination, aesthetic judgment, and sense of proportion. A few ideas:

· Wear a red leather belt and red pumps from the forties with a simple black dress or knit jumpsuit.
· Try a thirties straw hat with colored net as a wedding hat.
· Wear black Victorian lace-up boots with bright-colored stockings and a short skirt.
· Try 1920s satin T-strap or buckle-front shoes with the newest shorter trousers.
· Wear a large-brimmed straw hat on the beach with a short white chemise as a cover-up.
· Carry a 1950s gold or rhinestone-studded purse for evening, and wear gold kid thirties shoes and belt.

Prices

The going rate for vintage purses, shoes, belts, and hats varies so widely it's impossible to pinpoint. The following list will give you at least a vague idea of the range you can expect to pay; as usual, prices depend on condition, quality, detailing, uniqueness, and so forth.

Victorian and twenties shoes: $25–$150
1930s silver or gold kid shoes: $40–$100
Satin forties bed slippers: $40
Alligator or lizard shoes: $35–$100
Beaver or collapsible top hats: $50–$75
Very decorative cloche hats: $50–$125
Straw boaters and thirties brimmed hats: $25–$65
Thirties and forties felt hats with trim: $20–$75
Decorative leather and skin belts: $20–$75
Tooled cowboy belts: $12–$45
Hand-beaded Indian belts from the forties: $30–$50
Victorian beaded purses: $40–$350
Twenties metal mesh purses: $30–$150
Twenties and thirties leather clutch purses: $25–$200
Forties and fifties beaded clutch or pouch purses: $20–$100

18

Jewelry: Collectible Glitter, Wearable Funk

Only one thing wakes me up faster than a cup of coffee: someone telling me, "I have jewelry to sell." Since my first London buying trip for antique jewelry ten years ago, I have become an avid collector.

I buy and sell Art Deco Celluloid, chrome, and other interesting costume pieces, along with Victorian and silver thirties jewelry. Style and design are what I look for; my only other requirements: collectibility, excellent condition, and a bit of humor. Buy the best examples you can afford of a particular period. Buy the most nearly perfect condition, if possible; but don't reject a special or extraordinary piece if the damage is only slight.

If you're interested in buying expensive antique jewelry rather than inexpensive costume pieces, you should know as much about jewelry as possible. There are many books about collecting jewelry; study these before spending thousands of dollars. This chapter should give you some help and encourage you to read more.

Victorian Jewelry

Most people looking at "old" jewelry assume it's Victorian. This is the period that everyone has heard about and wants to collect. The small and delicate gold-filigree bar pins and rings of the Victorian era have been available for years at flea markets and antique shops in both England and the United States.

The Victorian era (1837–1900) was the first period in which jewelry was made for the common people as well as the aristocracy. Nine-karat and fifteen-karat gold ("pure" gold is twenty-four karat) was used for jewelry making in England; six-karat gold was used in the United States. Garnets, turquoises, and diamonds were the stones most often used with this lighter gold. Designs were symmetrical in oval, circular, and square shapes.

Victorian jewelry can be worn with clothes of

any period, as long as the "character," design, and color of the jewelry works with the clothes. For example: A little gold Victorian bar pin usually works well on a small-collared blouse, holding the two collar edges together. In groups of twos or threes, gold bar pins look great on a jacket lapel. Don't wear a simple gold bar pin on a jewel-neck cashmere sweater—it would get lost. Of course, Victorian jewelry also looks great accessorizing Victorian clothes. A bold oval pin set with almandine garnets is a beautiful accessory on a lace Victorian blouse or to hold the collar of a crepe dress closed.

The small, delicate, gold-and-stone rings from the Victorian period are very popular. On a pretty hand, many rings can be worn together; I have seen as many as six or seven grouped on one hand, and the look is still delicate, not "dramatic."—a nice way to show off a collection of antique gold rings.

Opposite top: *This Victorian bar pin of gold and small stones also works well as a lapel pin or at the neck of a thirties silk blouse.*

Opposite bottom left: *Victorian gold and seed pearl necklace and earrings on a scroll-link chain, circa 1875.*

Opposite bottom right: *Two pairs of American Victorian gold earrings; one set with topaz, the other with cabochon garnets.*

Above: *Diamond-and-ruby ring set in 14 karat gold from the late nineteenth century.*

Always buy Victorian jewelry from a reputable dealer. Original Victorian jewelry has no safety catch, so add a spring clutch (available at a jeweler's) for protection. Keep in mind that repairs or reworking (such as change of stones or transforming a necklace into pin and earrings) devalues antique jewelry. And be sure to find out whether you are buying 9-, 14-, 15-, or 22-karat gold. Look for poorly done repairs, cracks in metal, missing stones, and pieces that have been put together or taken apart; these are no longer "originals" and are consequently of less value. A reputable dealer should be able to tell you all of these things. Only then can you decide if you want to buy the piece. Prices depend on gold, gems, and age. They can start at $25 and go as high as $5000 and up. And costs are higher at auctions, shows, and shops that specialize in Victorian jewelry.

Art Nouveau

Art Nouveau jewelry (1890–1910), most of which was made in France and Germany (Victorian was the principal jewelry style of England), focused on figures, flowers, flowing hair, and faces. The most famous—and one of the finest—jewelry designers of this period was the French designer René Lalique, who worked with gold, glass, ivory, and semiprecious stones such as opals. Manufacturers of the period such as William Kerr, Unger Brothers, and George Shiebler—all American—used silver and enameling. Their techniques and styling made Art Nouveau pieces some of the most collectible and expensive jewelry you can buy. Much of it can be found in the United States today, because wealthy Americans who traveled in Europe between the wars brought Art Nouveau and Art Deco jewelry back to this country. After World War II much of this finer quality Nouveau jewelry could not be found in Europe. At that time Nouveau jewelry became highly prized for its design and workmanship. In England Murrle Bennett was part of an arts and crafts movement of hand-crafted jewelry that made use of silver, gold, pearls, amethysts, and turquoises. If you find any of this jewelry, buy it! It is among the best of this period.

Another famous innovator of the arts and crafts

Top: *Art Nouveau–style cameo pin—gold mount encasing a profile of a woman.*

A few very collectible pieces in silver and gold: (center) a silver Georg Jensen forties bracelet; (left, third row) a silver 1940s deer pin by Georg Jensen; (center, third row) a gold English Art Nouveau Murrle Bennett pin with rubies, blister-pearl center, and pearl drop; (right, third row) a turn-of-the-century silver cameo of Diana by Unger Brothers; (bottom) an Art Nouveau silver pin by Shiebler.

movement was Georg Jensen (from Denmark), whose silver jewelry and flatwear is still in great demand. Most of his work to be found today was made between the twenties and forties. Jensen's pins and bracelets still turn up at flea markets and antique shows—and at affordable prices. Finer quality Jensen pieces are hand-finished designs in silver. The work of many other Scandinavian designers from this period resembles Jensen designs but is cheaper to buy.

Jensen pins cost $100 and up; Jensen bracelets go for $150 and up.

Art Deco Jewelry

Everyone has heard of "Art Deco"—but what does it look like? Very often the words are used loosely to describe anything geometric. We can say with certainty that Radio City Music Hall is the epitome of Art Deco design. But what about jewelry: How do we recognize it? What's fun to collect? What's available—and where?

Although Art Deco design was strongly influenced by Cubism, ancient Egyptian art, and American Indian and Mexican design, it also reflected the streamlined machine age. The most common Art Deco motifs of sunrays, fountains, running deer, and nude women can be found on everything from a costly Lalique glass necklace (Lalique designed in the Art Deco style as well as Art Nouveau) to an inexpensive plastic Bakelite-and-chrome bracelet. Heavy silver Mexican jewelry made in the forties has a strong Art Deco influence. (Many jewelry dealers have begun to find Mexican silver and stone jewelry interesting; so keep your eye out for these tourist-travel cast-offs when you're shopping at flea markets or house sales.)

One of the best-known jewelry designers who worked during the Art Deco period was Louis Cartier. His precious stone and metal Art Deco jewelry is so highly prized and collectible that auctions including his jewelry often have standing room only. Other brilliant Art Deco jewelry designers include Boucheron, Fouquet, and Mauboussin from France. The silver, enamel, marcasite, and stone jewelry of the German designer Theodor Fahrner, though highly prized, is more affordable than the work of the French designers.

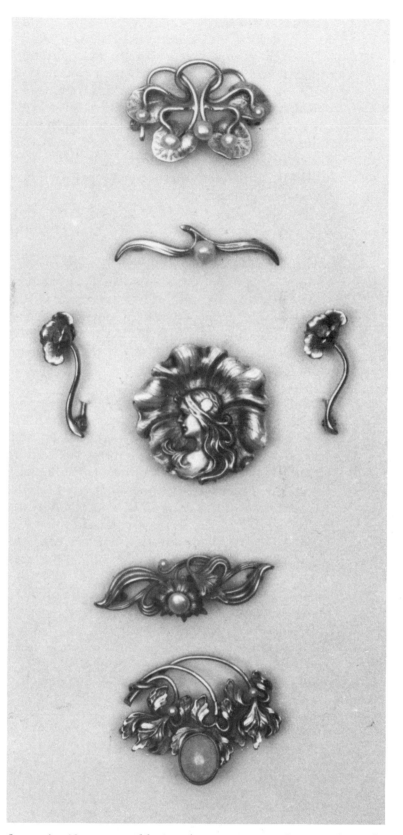

Seven Art Nouveau gold pins, featuring enameling, seed pearls, and small diamonds; American, circa 1900.

Some of the designs of the Art Deco period were translated into imitations—glass and plastic "kitsch" jewelry. A lovely paste or glass imitation of a real Art Deco diamond brooch can make a perfect accessory. It's often a bargain to buy, and you don't need an insurance policy before you wear it. Bakelite-and-chrome pieces done by imitators of the famous designers are also available at affordable prices. Remember: Style and design are what count—not whether you're wearing diamonds and platinum.

Marcasites

Marcasite jewelry from the 1930s is popular again and can even be found in some large department stores that usually sell only new jewelry. But prices are higher in department stores than they are in most antique stores or flea markets. Plus, the excitement of hunting down a perfect marcasite brooch is less when the shops are large and impersonal.

Much of the best marcasite jewelry was made in Germany and France. Look for good workmanship, sterling-silver settings, hand-set stones, and intricate design. Many of these brooches are initialed, but this should not stop you from purchasing a piece of jewelry. If someone in your family has an initialed pin she never wears, get it out and make use of it. To clean a marcasite pin, use cream silver polish on the back. Take special care cleaning the front of the pin where the stones are. An old soft toothbrush may be used with the cream silver polish. Then wash the cream off with water. If you lose any marcasites, these can easily be replaced by a jeweler at minimal cost.

Prices depend on quality and condition. Pins run from $40 to $250; rings, from $75 to $275. Necklaces range from $100 to $400; and bracelets go for $75 to $300.

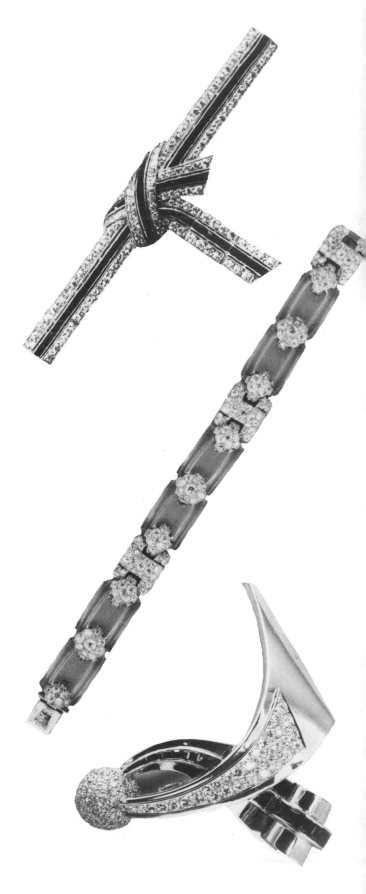

Top: *An Art Deco–stylized Tiffany and Company platinum-and-diamond brooch, circa 1925.* Center: *Art Deco crystal and diamond bracelet set in platinum and stamped "Cartier London."* Bottom: *A free-form Art Deco ruby-and-diamond brooch, in white and yellow gold, circa 1935.*

Opposite: *Paste-and-silver Deco pins of this type are readily available, inexpensive, and look good on the lapel of a tweed jacket.*

Right: *A paste necklace from the 1930s hand set in brass. The style is Hollywood's idea of Victoriana and is cheap elegance, lots of fun to wear at home with lingerie, with a black dressy suit, or, for real contrast, over a white Victorian high-necked blouse.*

Below: *A 1920s bracelet and ring of green onyx and marcasite set in silver, worn here with a printed-velvet twenties coat. This kind of jewelry can also be worn casually with sweaters, suits, and dresses.*

Opposite: *Assortment of Celluloid, silver, copper, and chrome: (left) silver-and-paste flower pin, copper bracelet, and Celluloid bangles; (center) black-and-yellow Celluloid necklace and chrome forties bean bracelet; (right) Celluloid clips in brown and amber, red and green Celluloid pins, and a plastic-and-rhinestone crescent pin.*

Good Plastic

Plastic, which includes Celluloid and Bakelite, has always been the least expensive jewelry, and its variety of colors and designs makes it wearable with any sporty outfit. A pair of carved red plastic clips, for example, makes an inexpensive accessory for a white linen jacket, which is how Jacqueline Bisset wore a pair purchased from me last year. A carved white plastic ring looks elegant on a tanned hand. Other ideas: a large carved plastic pin on a jacket or coat lapel or to hold a scarf in place; a dozen thin plastic bangle bracelets in a range of colors to wear with a plain black jersey dress; or a chunky white-and-gold Bakelite necklace at the neck of a simple cashmere sweater; four amber-colored bracelets with a rust-colored suede jacket.

Prices of plastic pins and clips range from $10 to $40; bracelets, $10 to $50; necklaces, $25 to $85.

Other Baubles

Copper jewelry made in Mexico and the United States is still cheap and widely available. If you like its color and can find interesting designs, think of it as an alternative to more expensive metals.

Silver pins from the thirties to fifties in all sizes and designs—from the more refined Georg Jensen designs to larger sculptural flower or leaf patterns—look great on jacket lapels and coat collars. Small versions look good at the neck of a small-collared blouse. Marcasite clips work well on a jacket pocket or can be turned into earrings.

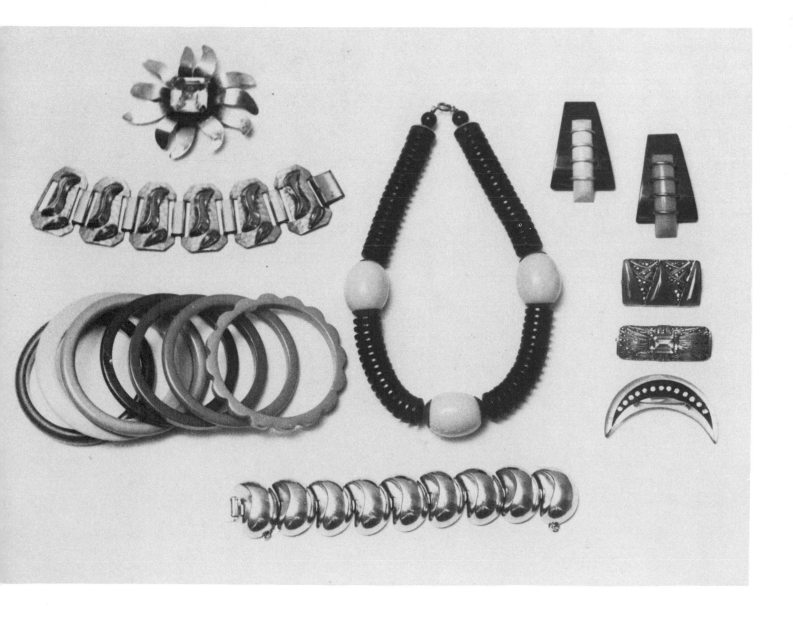

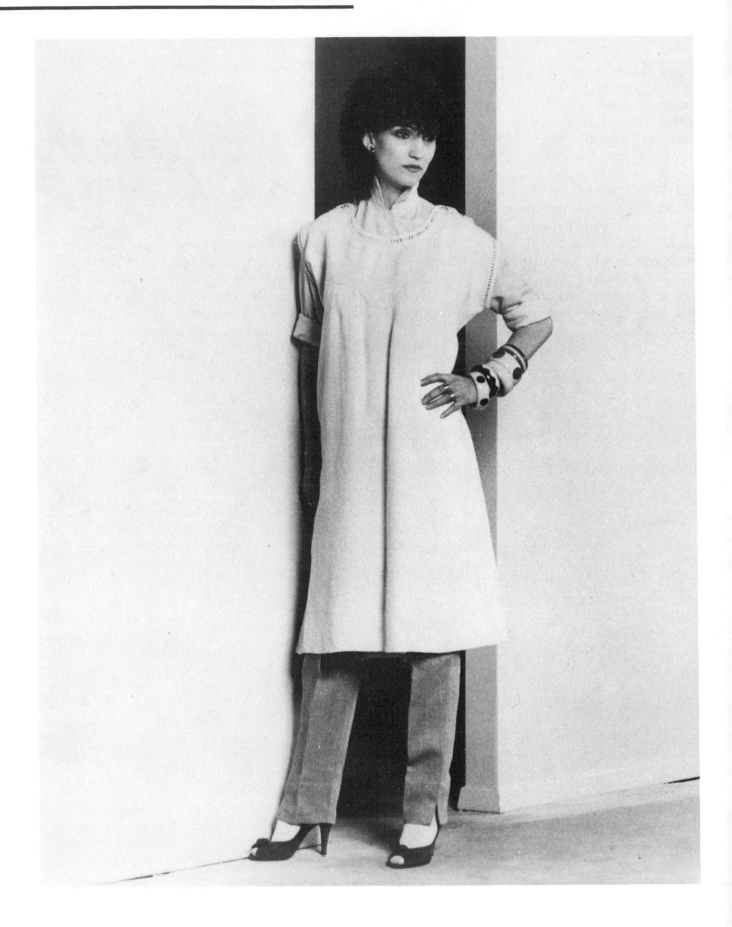

Opposite: *A collection of wide black-and-white Celluloid bangles works well with this beige linen chemise and straight pants because there are no other accessories to detract from the clean, simple lines of the outfit.*

Left: *Forties kitsch in sterling and blue glass worn here as a lapel pin. It could also make an interesting scarf pin or brighten the lapel or collar of a winter coat.*

If you enjoy wearing earrings and want expensive ones, pierce your ears. Screw-back styles often hurt the earlobe; clip-ons are easy to lose. Most screw-back styles can be converted for pierced ears. If you're thinking of piercing your ears, take my advice: Don't have a friend do it. See a professional.

Enameled-metal cuff links convert easily to earrings, and you even have an extra pair for a friend. Often these are much cheaper and easier to find than regular earrings. Be sure to put a 14-karat-gold post on the earrings when you convert them.

How to Wear and Care for Antique Jewelry

An antique necklace—whether it's delicately linked stones, chunky multicolored plastic, forties silver, Art Deco crystal and beads, or an enameled pendant—looks best when the neckline it's worn on is not too busy. The simpler the neckline, the more one can see an exquisite but small antique neckpiece. Often necklaces look even better worn on bare skin or under an open-necked blouse. Heavier, bolder pieces also work well with a bare neckline.

Bangle bracelets or metal-link bracelets look best in multiples of four or five. One of my customers is well known for her collection of over a hundred silver bracelets—all of which she seems to wear at the same time! Some people collect carved plastic bracelets in every color and wear six or seven on one arm for a special effect. Multiple bracelets look best on a bare arm or with a simple sleeve. Puffy, lacey sleeves don't work well with carved plastic bangle bracelets. Bold-looking wide bracelets made of metal and stone can work alone. Be sure that gold, silver, and semiprecious bracelets have safety chains and good clasps.

All faceted stones (such as diamonds) set in gold glitter after an ammonia bath. So does crystal. Clorox tarnishes silver in seconds—so never use it. And never use household cleansers for cleaning silver—they're too abrasive.

19

Making Things Fit

With antique clothes the size you see is the size you get, which explains one of the most frequent cries of distress of the vintage shopper: "Oh, this doesn't fit!" If it doesn't, please remember that having things altered usually works.

And if you sew, you know that one of the best things about doing it yourself is that you can make fast alterations cheaply while you watch television.

Despite the rumor that Americans are getting bigger all the time, there seems to be a surplus of larger sizes in most vintage clothes. So the question most often asked is, "Is there any way I can make this smaller—without having it totally taken apart and reassembled?"

Fast Tricks: Simple Ways to Make Clothes Smaller

Certain clothes lend themselves to fast little alteration tricks worked out by veteran old-clothes buyers who have a store of effective measures for sizing an overlarge dress or blouse or pair of pants. These instant alterations often give the garment more style than it had originally.

One caution: Neatness definitely counts. Simple as these sewing tips are, they have to be done right to bring off the look. Crookedness or kindergarten stitches do not work.

BELTS

Don't laugh: Recognizing which large dresses (and sometimes coats) can be magically paired with the right belt is a key skill. This trick works best with soft rayon print dresses of the forties. A size 12 dress with a softly fitted bodice and a slightly A-shaped skirt can often be belted into a dress with a blouson top and gathered skirt for a size 8 figure with no further changes. The belt trick is most successful with fabrics that are thin enough to be gathered at the waist without bunching up. If you don't happen to be wearing a belt when you go shopping, most store people will be happy to lend you one for trying on. A narrow elastic belt works very well, because it clings to you *and* to the dress, holding everything together with less sliding than a leather belt.

Watch what happens as you move around; raise your arms and sit down. If the waistline wanders above and below the belt as you move, causing an uneven hemline and an uneven amount of blousiness on the top, add belt loops or more belt loops. One loop at each side seam is usual, but you may need more. The easiest and most unobstructive are thread loops. To make them, choose a heavy sewing thread or button thread in the appropriate color (go too dark rather than too light) and braid a little string that's long enough for the belt to pass through plus an extra inch. Tack it to the waistline with a couple of invisible stitches. If the thread is thin, make each of the three braiding strands from two, three, or four pieces of thread.

Many women turn men's shirts into a great look for themselves by wearing them belted with shirttails out. Wear the shirt with lots of buttons undone; it underlines the sexiness of a woman in men's clothing. Or create a jacketlike effect by wearing another shirt or blouse underneath. The collar and lapels of the inner shirt should be worn over the top shirt; try turning up both collars in back.

SHOULDER PADS

Drooping shoulders can drag down the look of a blouse or dress even if the body of the garment looks good hanging loose. If the shoulders are only moderately big, try putting in a pair of new shoulder pads. You can buy them in the notions sections of dime stores or department stores. Shoulder pads come in different sizes and materials, but the most widely available are triangular-shaped fabric-covered foam rubber. To position them, attach the middle of the base of one triangular pad to the point where the shoulder seam meets the sleeve, the apex of the triangle to the shoulder seam near the neck; tack down the two other points to the sleeve seam in front and back

Shoulder pads.

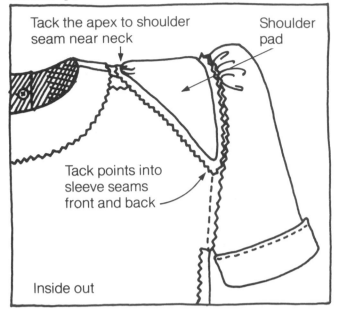

of the shoulder (see illustration). Anchor the pads at the seams so the tack won't pull at the material and show from the outside. Before you sew, pin the pads into place with straight pins and study the effect in the mirror; don't forget the back view. You may have to reposition the pads a little to get the right effect. If the pads are too big, cut them to size and baste the edges together. If they're too small; use two pairs for more fatness. If you're inspired to make your own, think of them as little pot holders. Dacron batting is the ideal stuffing because it's less rigid than foam.

Getting the Shoulders Right

Assuming you've belted the dress, and that it works fine for the waist, what do you do if the shoulders are still too big? (Shoulder pads don't always work, especially if the dress is so large that the pads don't take up enough of the slack.) Or if you've found the Hawaiian shirt of your dreams but it seems to have belonged to a fullback? Or if the tweed in that man's coat is too good to pass up?

First, locate the shoulder seam—the seam that joins the front and back of the garment together or joins the front to the back yoke. Put on the garment, stand in front of a mirror with some straight pins within reach, and try out the following methods to get the shoulders to fit. Once the shoulders are right, the eye will accept the bodice fullness as a style rather than a mistake.

SHOULDER GATHERS FOR SOFT TOPS

With soft fabric draw the material into tiny, even little waves along the shoulder seam until the sleeve top is brought up to the right place. Any excess fullness should fall softly, close to the body. (If the fabric is heavy, it will stick out stiffly and the shoulder will appear lumpy.) To gather: Using heavy-duty thread, or a double strand of regular thread, make a secure knot on the inside at one end of the shoulder seam. Then take tiny, neat, even stitches along the seam line on the *outside*; make your stitches as invisible as possible by following exactly the original seam (see illustration). When you get to the other end of the seam, draw the thread tight, pushing and arranging the fabric into even gathers. Try on the garment again to decide how narrow to make the shoulder. Then tie off the thread on the underside with another big knot. Even though the material could theoretically gather up unevenly along the thread, it usually doesn't; so don't worry about it. But check it when you iron or when you get it back from the cleaners.

Gathering the shoulders.

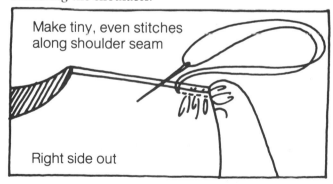

Make tiny, even stitches along shoulder seam

Right side out

TUCKS FOR SHIRTS

With a big shirt you can take one, two, or three small- to medium-sized pleats or tucks (half an inch to two inches wide) at the shoulder seam on each side of the front, as illustrated. Tucks gener-

ally look best pointing away from the face toward the sleeve. Be sure both sides are symmetrical.

For a softer look:

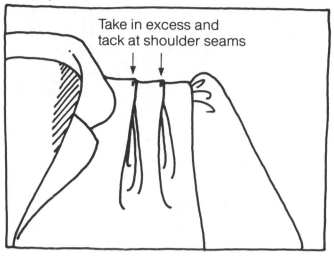

Take in excess and tack at shoulder seams

FANCY SEWN-IN PLEATS

The hardest but best-looking pleat treatment for blouses, dresses, and sometimes light coats is a series of vertical seams that lie over your shoulders like half-moons. They run two to three inches down from the shoulder seams in front and back and can be longer in front than in back, depending on what looks best.

The number of seams and the amount of material to be taken up depends on how small you want the garment to be. Many small tucks usually

For a tailored feeling:

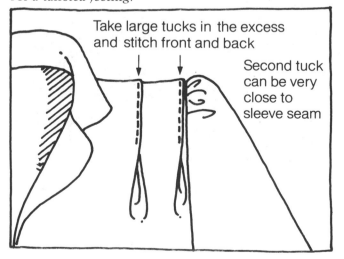

Take large tucks in the excess and stitch front and back

Second tuck can be very close to sleeve seam

The single large pleat at the edge of the shoulder of this tweed man's coat of the fifties makes it fit perfectly and adds a nice detail. The pleat or fold has been sewn down very securely at the waist as well.

look better than a few big ones. Do the tucking with the extra material on the inside for a more tailored look, or leave it on the outside to create a nice detail of little puffed rows of fabric. You can leave the tucks unpressed for fullness, or iron the fabric into pleats. Make sure the seams are evenly separated and equal in length. They *must* be neat for this trick to work. Once again: You've made the shoulders fit, given fullness to the body of the garment, and added nice detailing.

THE SINGLE-BIG-FOLD METHOD FOR DRESSES AND COATS

You can take the same little tucks on a dress as on a blouse, but it's often better to take one large fold—using enough fabric to bring the shoulder seam to the right place, on each side, either along the shoulder line (see photograph) or between the shoulder and the neck. Repeat the same tuck at the waist. This gives you a graceful, falling, panel effect. This style is especially good if you have big shoulders (or wear shoulder pads) and is also good for a small bust.

With coats one large pleat at the edge of the shoulder usually works best—if a trick like this works at all. Tucking creates a beautifully sculptural effect, either when the coat is falling free or when it's belted. If it's belted, tack the pleat at the waist, too, so it will be folded correctly under the belt. Do this alteration first; then shorten or lengthen the cuffs if necessary, because the former alteration will pull them up somewhat. If you're changing the hem, always do that last.

Tricks with Trousers

Simple pleats at the waist can make large men's pants into fashionably loose pleated trousers in minutes (see illustration). Of course, the best you can get in just a few minutes is pleats in the waistband, which does not look as finished as pants that have been conventionally altered by removing and resetting the waistband. But the quick method provides a perfectly good look for the few minutes' time you've invested.

If you want to peg pants legs, alter the *outside* leg seam at the cuff. One method (see illustra-

To take in pants at the waist, pin out excess, try on, and stitch pleats.

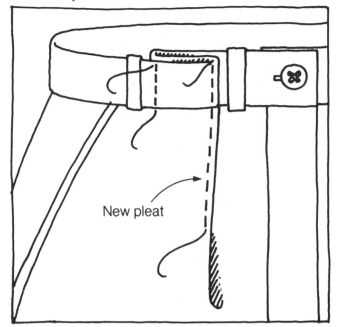

New pleat

To taper pants at hem.

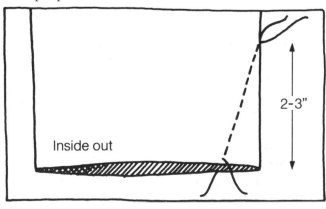

Inside out

2-3"

For tapered or pegged pants with an exterior pleat: Make an inverted pleat at pants hem and tack with a few stitches.

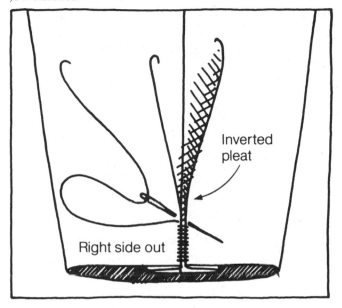

Inverted pleat

Right side out

tion): Turn the leg inside out and proceed as if you were going to make the whole leg narrower—but sew only one or two inches. This gives a band effect at the bottom of the leg. Another method: Working on the outside of the pants leg, make an inverted pleat at the side seam and tack it together with a few stitches (see illustration). Or use snaps at the cuff; that way, you can have the option of pegged or regular legs.

If you are thin and of average height, you can wear suspenders with large men's pants and let them hang loose around the waist. You can also hike up the waistline with the suspenders, bring-

ing the crotch of the pants to the proper position but letting the waistband hover around your rib cage. It doesn't matter if that makes the pants legs quite short—short pants look good with this shape. (David Bowie wore pants like this at a concert once and *he* looked wonderful.)

Skirt Waistbands

A gathered skirt that's too big can sometimes be fixed by inserting a couple of pleats at the waist rather than by removing and resetting the waistband. If you have to wear a new skirt the day you buy it, you can usually get away with it by lapping the waistband over and pinning the gathered portion with an interesting pin as a temporary measure. To alter a waistband, take one medium or two small tucks on each side in the front. This method works only if the material is soft enough to drape rather than bunch and bulge.

The Old-fashioned Drawstring

Many teddies and camisoles were made with an adjustable drawstring along the top just above the bust. Very sensible, and an idea you may be able to adapt. There may be a ready-made space created by the top hem of the camisole, or you could sew a piece of ribbon or seam tape on the underside of the top to make a channel through which to string a narrow ribbon. You can tie the string on the inside. Or make a buttonhole-type opening in center front, so the bow can show out.

The drawstring concept is also applicable to certain skirts. It probably works best on Victorian white petticoats. String a ribbon through the waistband and tie it at the side. If you are making a skirt by cutting off the top of a dress, sew a little channel on top as if you were making space for a curtain rod, and thread it with ribbon.

Side Seams and Darts

If you've never really looked at the *inside* of a dress, you may be surprised to realize that the side seam of a dress or blouse is very often just one long row of stitching beginning at the cuff of the sleeve and running up and around the armpit and down the side to the shirttail or dress hem. If there is no side closing, you can make a garment a

Side seam alterations.

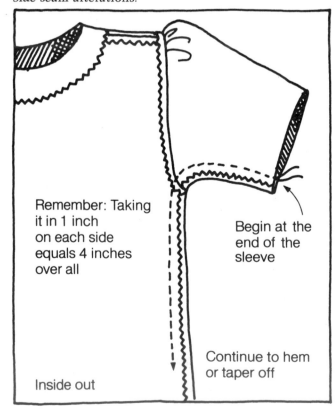

Remember: Taking it in 1 inch on each side equals 4 inches over all

Begin at the end of the sleeve

Continue to hem or taper off

Inside out

lot smaller very easily with two simple machine seams, one down each side (see illustration). Don't attempt a hand-stitched seam unless you know how to do a fine seam. And remember that taking a *one-inch*-deep seam on each side makes the whole garment *four* inches smaller. Don't forget: You can make the seam a little wider here and narrower there. And if it's a dress with a button opening at the waist, don't make the waist so small that you can't get the dress over your head. Take up waist slack with a belt.

Darts.

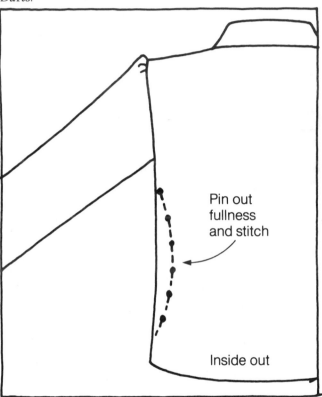

Pin out fullness and stitch

Inside out

The word *dart* may make your eyes glaze over because it sounds like something only to be pronounced by a professional tailor. But it's possible, on certain clothes, to alter them by adding a dart or two. An unlined jacket, or almost any dress, can be nipped in at a vertical seam. Or you can take it in by sewing a very tapered boomerang-shaped dart on the wrong side of the garment (see illustration). Keep darts modest; a little dart can work wonders removing a droopy, baggy look; but big darts usually look home-made—because they leave too much fabric bulging above and below the dart. Darts have to be tapered at the ends very gradually and to a point.

Hems, Sleeve Lengths, and Buttons

A change in skirt length can totally alter how a garment looks. If you are making any other alterations, save hemming until last, because other changes may hike the skirt up.

Sleeves that are too long can be dealt with in several ways other than removing the cuff to shorten the sleeve. You can move the button to make the cuff fit more tightly, leaving pretty fullness falling around the wrist. Or you can machine sew a pleat or two around the circumference of the sleeve near the cuff, leaving the fabric fold on the outside (see illustration).

If a short-sleeved garment looks frumpy, try shortening the sleeve. They are easy to fix, and an inch or two can make a dramatic difference in the whole proportion of the top, especially a big one that you are belting or tucking. Short sleeves that are too long can look dowdy; shortening them, even if they are wide, can really perk a shirt up. Either hem them, or make a cuff if there is enough fabric.

If buttons are missing, look around to see if there is one under the collar that you'll never use. Sometimes there are two on a long-sleeved shirt cuff where one would go. Or steal the cuff buttons (if they are the same size) to replace those in front. If you can't match the buttons, the cuffs are far enough away that no one will notice slightly different ones there. Or you can replace all the buttons. This is not a major task. In fact, you might want to consider it anyway; it's one way to improve a garment—and the reason flea-market shoppers always pick up great old buttons just in case. Last tip: Always save buttons from clothes you are consigning to the rag heap. They may come in handy.

The Tailor

Clothes that almost fit can be taken in or let out at the seams by the tailor at your dry cleaner, if they have one, or by a local dressmaker or tailor. Of course, tailors also do hems, cuffs, zippers, and buttons. If you are having a major alteration done, you may need a preliminary fitting. In fact, you might want to insist on it.

To shorten sleeves: Take a tuck or two and sew.

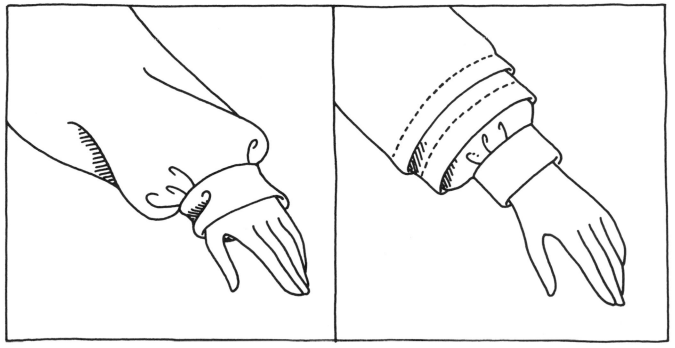

It's a good idea to find out which alterations are easy and which are difficult or expensive to do, and keep this in mind when you are shopping for clothes. For example: Resetting a sleeve, which means taking it out, making the sleeve and armhole smaller, and raising the shoulder seam, sounds like an impossible task to the nonsewer, but it is, in fact, very simple for a tailor. On the other hand, tackling lapels and necklines is usually very complicated. If the lapels are too wide for you, or if the collar is too long, don't purchase the garment. Reshaping those parts of a jacket or coat is almost impossible. After a little chat with a tailor, you'll be able to assess more accurately whether something can be altered at all and if the coat is worth it.

PART THREE

Store Listings

Arizona

SCOTTSDALE

Dynabell's
3704 North Scottsdale Road
Scottsdale, AZ 85251
602–941–2969
Hours: Mon.–Sat., 10–6
Owner: Dyanne Silver
Large store with selection from Victorian to fifties in varied condition. Lots of kimonos.

California

BERKELEY

Few and Far
1510 Walnut Street
Berkeley, CA 94609
415–845–8333
Hours: Mon.–Sat., 11–5:30
Owner: Jesse Russell
Small boutique with mostly women's vintage clothing from the 1940s plus kimonos and some new accessories, such as hats, with a 1930s feeling.

LOS ANGELES

Crystal Palace
8435 Melrose Avenue
Los Angeles, CA 90069
213–653–6148
Hours: Mon.–Fri., 11–5; Sat., 1–5
Owner: Robert Becker
A vintage-clothing old standby, mostly for women, with Edwardian whites through 1950s glamour. Lovely accessories.

Memories
8302 West Third Street
Los Angeles, CA 90048
213–655–4749
Hours: Mon.–Sat., 11:30–5:30
Owner: Mike Dykeman
A tasteful and eclectic vintage selection (fashion oriented, always changing) from the 1930s to the 1950s for men and women. Hawaiian shirts, pants, jackets, coats, dresses, and funky accessories at moderate prices with friendly service.

Paleeze
708 North Curzon
Los Angeles, CA 90046
213–653–6359
Hours: Tues.–Sat., 1–6
Owner: Karl Holm
A selection of vintage clothing, mostly from the 1940s and 1950s. Hawaiian shirts, jackets, dresses, blouses, pants, and a colorful array of costume jewelry.

Repeat Performance
7261 Melrose Avenue
Los Angeles, CA 90046
213–938–0609
Hours: Mon.–Sat., 11–6
Owner: Jean Gold
A tastefully edited vintage-clothing store with Edwardian whites as well as special Hawaiian shirts, dresses, jackets, and fun accessories. Friendly service, stylish windows, fashion oriented.

Straight Jacket
8046 West Third Street
Los Angeles, CA 90048
213–658–8190
Hours: Mon.–Sat., 11:30–5:30
Owner: Name unavailable
Varied clothing from the 1950s and 1960s for men and women.

NORTH HOLLYWOOD

La Rue
5320 Lankershim Boulevard
North Hollywood, CA 91601
213–762–2072
Hours: Mon.–Sat., 10:30–5:30
Owners: Chris Moore and Joan Prieto
A large store stocked with daytime and evening wear mostly from 1940 to 1960 for men and women. Good Hawaiian and cowboy shirts have been located here. A friendly atmosphere.

OAKLAND

Second Time Around
351 17th Street
Oakland, CA 94612
415–465–3449
Hours: Mon.–Fri., 12–6; Sat., 12–4
Owner: Debra Grady
Vintage clothing mostly from the 1930s to 1950s, including tuxedos, Hawaiians, and shoes for men, and dresses, suits, hats, and furs for women. Fashion shows

and fashion consulting is done by the manager, J. W. Welzcher. Costume rentals also.

PASADENA

Rosy Memories
21 East Holly Street
Pasadena, CA 91103
213-449-0108
Hours: Mon.-Sat., 11-5
Owner: John Strawss
Vintage clothing from the 1930s and 1940s for men and women. Mostly day wear; also collectibles, pottery, and lots of jewelry.

Sugar Daddy's
18 South Fairoaks
Pasadena, CA 91105
203-793-3532
Hours: Mon.-Sat., 11-6
Owners: Van Stewart and David Packard
A well-styled store with vintage clothing from the 1920s to the 1950s for men and women. Art Deco collectibles and accessories add to its pulled-together look.

SAN DIEGO

Buffalo
1451 Garnet Avenue
San Diego, CA 92109
714-270-2031
Hours: Mon.-Sat., 10:30-6:00
Owner: Name unavailable
A selection of men's and women's vintage clothing in varied condition from the 1940s and 1950s. Open since 1971.

Deju Vu
3748 Park Boulevard
San Diego, CA 92103
714-293-7355
Hours: Mon.-Sat., 12:00-5:30
Owner: Philip Auey
Mostly day clothing such as bowling shirts, tweed jackets, and gabs for men and rayon dresses for women.

Mixed Produce
1475 University Avenue
San Diego, CA 92103
714-692-9927
Hours: Mon.-Fri., 11-7; Sat., 10-7
Owners: Michael Reams and Arnold Aquilar
Men's and women's vintage clothing mostly from the 1930s to the 1950s.

Wear It Again Sam
3922 Park Boulevard
San Diego, CA 92103
714-299-0185
Hours: Mon.-Sat., 11-6
Owner: Kriss Bennett
Vintage clothing for men and women—gabardine shirts, men's tweed jackets, pants, rayon dresses, blouses, and women's wool jackets.

SAN FRANCISCO

The Best of Everything
2121 Fillmore Street
San Francisco, CA 94115
415-563-2378
Hours: Mon.-Sat., 11-6
Owner: Lorraine Wohl
Large, nicely edited shop for women's clothing and jewelry. Edwardian whites, 1930s dresses, lingerie, and accessories in a charming atmosphere with friendly service.

Grand Illusion
1604 Union Street
San Francisco, CA 94123
415-673-3136
Hours: Mon.-Sat., 10:30-6:30; Fri., 10:30-7:00
Owner: Jet Brooks
Large shop with men's and women's clothing from 1900 to the 1950s. Some never-worn clothing. Formal-wear rentals.

Hot Stuff
1128 Polk Street
San Francisco, CA 94109
415-885-1982
Hours: Mon.-Sat., 11:30-7:00
Owners: Thomas Faville and Brian Federow
A well-edited selection of clothing from the 1920s through the 1950s for men and women. Good Hawaiian shirts, some whites.

Masquerade
2237 Union Street, Second Floor
San Francisco, CA 94123
415-567-5677
Hours: Mon.-Sat., 11-6; Sun., 1-5
Owner: Shawn Bradwin
A tasteful and edited selection for men and women, including Hawaiian shirts, dresses, sweaters, and funky jewelry. Lovely window displays and friendly service.

Matinee
1124 Polk Street
San Francisco, CA 94109
415-673-6145
Hours: Daily, 12-6
Owners: David Tarbet and David Gillette
A fully packed store with men's and women's vintage clothing mostly from the 1940s to the 1950s. Stock includes Hawaiians, pants and jackets for men, and lots of fifties clothing for women. Good service.

Old Gold Men's
2380 Market Street
San Francisco, CA 94114
415-522-4788
Hours: Mon.-Fri., 11:30-6:30; Sat., 12-6
Owners: Joseph Dubois and Dennis Mitchell
A well-merchandised men's vintage-clothing store with tasteful displays. Hawaiian shirts, pants, jackets, coats, accessories, and some new clothing. Good service.

Old Gold Women's
2319 Market Street
San Francisco, CA 94114
415-552-2560
Hours: Mon.-Fri., 11:30-6:30; Sat., 12-6
Owners: Joseph Dubois and Dennis Mitchell
Only women's clothing from the 1940s through the 1960s, well displayed in a small store. Lots of sweaters, jackets, dresses, and accessories.

Painted Lady
1838 Divisadero Street
San Francisco, CA 94115
Hours: Mon.-Sat., 11-6
Owner: Diane Breivis
Fun, tasteful store with mostly women's clothing from 1900 to 1950. Jackets, blouses, dresses, and accessories in a friendly atmosphere.

Pauli's Fantasy Clothes
400 Broadway
San Francisco, CA 94133
415-781-7233
Hours: Mon.-Sat., 12-7
Owner: Pauli Potter
Very large store stocked with women's dresses, blouses, and kimonos. Great plastic jewelry and some new clothing made with old fabric. Nice owner.

Sugar Tit
1474 Haight Street
San Francisco, CA 94117
415-552-7027

Hours: Mon.-Sat., 11-6
Owner: Alex McMath
Small and interesting selection of men's and women's clothing and accessories. Some furniture and collectibles too in this tiny shop. Nice service.

SANTA BARBARA

Easy Street
505 State Street
Santa Barbara, CA 93104
805-966-2803
Hours: Mon.-Wed., 12-5; Thurs. and Fri., 12-9
Owner: Pam Gensler
A nice shop with men's and women's vintage clothing, accessories, and jewelry. Mostly day wear, in varied condition.

Narcissus
507 Brinkerhoff
Santa Barbara, CA 93101
805-965-4082
Hours: Tues.-Sat., 12-5
Owner: Name unavailable
In business for fifteen years and devoted to Victorian and Edwardian clothing and accessories, including gowns, jewelry, and purses.

Pure Gold
718 State Street
Santa Barbara, CA 93101
805-962-4613
Hours: Mon.-Sat., 10-7; Sun., 12-5
Owners: Michael Mundy and Julia Hoffman
Vintage clothing from the 1940s and 1950s for men and women, well displayed. Evening and day wear, some Hawaiians; varied condition.

Yellowstone Clothing Co.
6551 Trigo Street
Santa Barbara, CA 93017
805-968-3617
Hours: Mon.-Sat., 10-6; Sun., 11-5
Owner: Paul Haugen
A romantic shop with women's clothing, accessories, and jewelry. Some linens, too, in varied condition. Interesting fixtures.

SANTA MONICA

Jadis
2701 Main Street
Santa Monica, CA 90405
213-396-3477

Hours: Wed.–Sat., 10:30–5:00; Sun., 12:30–5:00
Owners: Parke Meek and Susan Lieberman
A tasteful selection of mostly women's clothing from Edwardian whites and thirties dresses and lingerie to forties suits. These combined with newly made Deco sofas in a friendly atmosphere. Knowledgeable service.

VENICE

Choux
1505 West Washington Boulevard
Venice, CA 90291
213–396–0166
Hours: Mon.–Sat., 12–6
Owner: Chrystal Smithline
Men's and women's clothing from the 1950s and 1960s with a new wave look. Funky, good taste, and nice service.

Golyester
1356 West Washington Boulevard
Venice, CA 90291
213–396–7429
Hours: Mon.–Fri., appt. only; Sat., 12–5
Owner: Esther Ginsberg
A large selection of laces with some Edwardian antique and ethnic clothing. Some trim and jewelry.

Palace Museum
1239 West Washington Boulevard
Venice, CA 90291
213–399–9442
Hours: Mon.–Sat., 11–6; Sun., 12–5
Owner: Roland Tirelle
Moderately priced, orderly store for men and women. Tasteful, wearable clothing from the 1950s and 1960s; casual and friendly atmosphere.

Colorado

BOULDER

Golden Oldies
2027 Broadway
Boulder, CO 80302
303–449–0462
Hours: Mon.–Sat., 10–6
Owners: Patti and Scott Roche
Vintage clothing for men, women, and children, covering the decades from 1880 to 1950. Almost everything cleaned and mended. Large shop.

DENVER

The Ritz
1415 Larimer Street
Denver, CO 80202
303–572–9072
Hours: Mon.–Sat., 10–10; Sun., 12–6
Owner: Mark Alexander
Victorian and Edwardian whites, gabardine cowboy shirts, men's pleated pants and jackets. New futuristic clothing and paper products.

Connecticut

CANAAN

Lisa C.
Route 44 West
Canaan, CT 06018
203–824–7952
Hours: Mon.–Sun., 10–5
Owner: Lisa Consolini
A mixture of vintage clothing, accessories, and jewelry mostly for women; plus attic junk and furniture at high prices. Friendly owner.

NEWINGTON

The Doll Factory
2551 Berlin Turnpike
Newington, CT 06111
203–666–6162
Hours: Tues.–Sat., 1–6:30; Thurs.,1:00–8:30
Owner: Louise Schinelli
Clothing mostly from the 1950s and 1960s in varied condition. Some clothing and accessories from earlier decades.

District of Columbia

WASHINGTON

As Time Goes By
655 C Street, S.E.
Washington, DC 20003
202–543–7877
Hours: Tues.–Sat., 12–6
Owner: Susan Lihn
Small store for mostly women's clothing with some Edwardian whites plus a variety from other eras.

Broadway Baby
1641 Wisconsin Avenue, N.W.
Washington, DC 20007
202-338-7355
Hours: Tues.–Sat., 10–6
Owner: Rosanna Cohen
Men's and women's vintage clothing from the fifties, including pointy-toed shoes, prom dresses, suits, coats, and some furs.

Jamison and Hawkins
3061½ M Street, N.W.
Washington, DC 20007
202-965-6911
Hours: Mon.–Sat., 11–7
Owners: Carol Hawkins Franks and Henry Jamison Cord
Tastefully selected women's vintage clothing including Victorian, Edwardian whites, plus evening wear from the 1920s and 1930s. Clothing is cleaned and repaired. Helpful owners, lovely atmosphere.

Unforgettables
1083 Thomas Jefferson Street, N.W.
Washington, DC 20007
202-965-5644
Hours: Mon.–Sat., 11–6
Owner: Angela Kuff
A small basement boutique with mostly women's vintage clothing from 1900 to the 1950s, neatly displaycd, cleaned, and repaired. Whites in summer.

Florida

COCONUT GROVE

Nostalgia
3434A Main Highway
Coconut Grove, FL 33133
305-445-6498
Hours: Mon.–Sat., 10–6
Owner: Evelyn Rubin
Lovely, expensive collection of whites in lace and cotton. Good bridal source. Some beaded dresses and Oriental robes.

FORT LAUDERDALE

Glad Rags
209 South West Second Street
Fort Lauderdale, FL 33304

305-462-2996
Hours: Mon.–Sat., 10:30–5:00
Owner: Dani Senatore
Small boutique, half women's vintage clothing from 1900 to the 1950s, half new clothing.

GAINESVILLE

Persona
919 West University Avenue
Gainesville, FL 32601
904-372-0455
Hours: Mon.–Sat., 10–6
Owners: Nava Ottenberg, Barbara Biggins, and Harriet Roth
Vintage clothing for men and women mixed with new clothing and collectibles.

Play It Again
1636 West University Avenue
Gainesville, FL 32601
904-376-4080
Hours: Tues.–Sat., 12:00–5:30
Owners: Chris Carpenter, Peter Carpenter, and Ruth Gunderson
Small boutique with a selection of vintage clothing for men and women, mostly 1940s and 1950s. Some new accessories.

KEY WEST

Fonda's
111 Duval Street
Key West, FL 33040
305-294-5929
Hours: Daily, 10:30–8:30
Owner: Fonda
A selection for women of forties dresses, lingerie, Edwardian whites, and some accessories. Some Hawaiian shirts for men.

ST. AUGUSTINE

Pamela's Reminiscence
14D Saint George Street
St. Augustine, FL 32084
904-824-3231
Hours: Mon.–Sun., 11–5
Owner: Pamela McDonald
Small boutique with mostly women's vintage clothing; Edwardian whites and dressy clothes from the 1880s to the 1950s are the specialty.

Georgia

ATLANTA

Puttin' on the Ritz
3099 Peachtree Road
Atlanta, GA 30305
404-262-2224
Hours: Mon.–Sat., 12–7
Owners: Dana Moore and Debbi Boyd
Old and new clothing for men and women. Old clothing often in never-worn condition, including pleated pants, suits, and shoes.

Illinois

CHICAGO

B. H. Ltd. (Briar House)
843 West Armitage Avenue
Chicago, IL 60614
312-528-5145
Hours: Daily, 11–6
Owners: James L. Hernick and Clyde C. Smith
A collection of women's cocktail and dressy clothing from 1850 to 1950; accessories too. Some jewelry, collectibles, and kitsch. Good service.

Blake
614 West Belmont
Chicago, IL 60657
312-477-3364
Hours: Tues.–Fri., 1–7; Sat., 11–6
Owners: Marilyn Blafzka and Dominick Marcheschi
Small, spare stock, tastefully selective of women's clothing only, from 1890 to the 1950s. Nice service.

Blondie's White Rose Salon
2550 Clark Street
Chicago, IL 60614
312-549-6622
Hours: Tues.–Sat., 11–6
Owners: Edward and Adrienne Katien
Two shops in one space; one specializing in wedding dresses mostly from 1870 to 1920, and the other in evening wear from the 1920s to the 1960s. Some accessories and collectibles.

Kitch
1007 West Webster
Chicago, IL 60614
312-327-9665

Hours: Tues.–Fri., 1–8; Sat. and Sun., 1–6
Owners: David Jameson, Joan Riise, and Gloria McCartney
Period men's and women's fashions mostly from the 1930s to the 1950s, intermingled with art, collectibles, and furnishings. A stylish and interesting store.

Silver Moon
3337 North Halsted Street
Chicago, IL 60657
312-883-0222
Hours: Mon.–Sat., 12:30–6:30; Sun., 1–4
Owner: Tari Costan
A personally selected stock, mostly for women, from the 1890s to the 1950s. Some tuxedos and gabardine shirts for men. Nice service, interesting all-white décor.

Ziggurat
3420 North Halsted Street
Chicago, IL 60657
312-327-7787
Hours: Tues.–Fri., 12–7; Sat., 11–5
Owners: Lawson Skala and Don Gower
Victorian to 1940s clothes mostly for women—dressy as well as day clothes, plus accessories. Some men's pants and gabardine shirts.

WINNETKA

The Shirt Off Her Back
378 Greenbay Road
Winnetka, IL 60093
312-446-5524
Hours: Mon., Wed., Fri., 12–5; Tues., Thurs., Sat., 10:30–4:30
Owners: Sharon Dankoff and Linda Garfield
A selection of Victorian and Edwardian clothing, along with Queen Victoria memorabilia, linens, laces, and furniture.

Kentucky

COVINGTON

Garbo's
641 Main Strasse
Covington, KY 41011
606-291-9023
Hours: Daily, 12–5
Owner: Mary Lynne Finch
Men's and women's clothing mostly from 1920 to the 1950s including new wave looks. Also furniture and collectibles in this six-room shop.

Louisiana

NEW ORLEANS

Fleur de Paris
712 Royal Street
New Orleans, LA 70116
504–525–1899
Hours: Daily, 10–6
Owners: Randy Powell and Joseph Parrino
Elegant vintage clothing and accessories (about a third). The rest of the stock is custom millinery and contemporary clothing.

Matilda
1222 Decatur Street
New Orleans, LA 70116
504–524–7027
Hours: Thurs.–Mon., 12–5
Owner: JoAnn Clevenger
A large store with a thrift-shop atmosphere. Some theatrical clothing and Mardi Gras masks too.

Maine

AUBURN

Orphan Annie's
96 Court Street
Auburn, ME 04210
207–782–0638
Hours: Mon.–Sat., 10–5; Sun., 12–5
Owner: Daniel Poulin
Vintage clothing plus jewelry, home accessories, and some furniture from 1900 to the 1950s.

Maryland

BALTIMORE

Johanna
1047 South Charles Street
Baltimore, MD 21230
301–539–1917
Hours: Wed.–Sat., 11–7
Owner: Johanna Hoch
A very nice store, well stocked with rayon dresses from the forties and fifties, beaded sweaters and dresses, men's shirts, accessories, hats, shoes, and some Victorian and new custom clothing.

Massachusetts

BOSTON

Forever Flamingo
285 Newbury Street
Boston, MA 02115
617–267–2547
Hours: Mon.–Sat., 11–7
Owner: Barry Swartz
Art Deco collectibles, varied vintage clothing, and jewelry tastefully chosen by a delightful proprietor.

High Society
273 Newbury Street
Boston, MA 02116
617–266–8957
Hours: Mon.–Sat., 11–7
Owners: Ellie and Mark Ostrovsky
Formal vintage clothing from the 1940s, 1950s, and 1960s with a new wave look. Some new clothing.

Silver Threads
189 North Street
Boston, MA 02113
617–523–2360
Hours: Wed.–Sat., 11–7; Sun., 1–5
Owner: Debbi Shapiro
An eclectic mix of clothing, jewelry, and accessories for men and women, chosen with care and knowledge by a lovely owner.

GLOUCESTER

Bananas
11 Bass Avenue
Gloucester, MA 01930
617–283–8806
Hours: Thurs.–Sun., 12–5
Owner: Richard Leonard
Vintage clothing from the forties, fifties, and sixties with a funky flair. Owner also produces wild and theatrical fashion shows with his ever-changing stock.

LANSBORO

Yesterday's General Store
Route 7, South Main Street
Lansboro, MA 01237
413–443–5863
Hours: Daily, 10–6
Owners: Karen Bangs and Carol Yarmosky
Clothing and furniture in a country atmosphere.

Women's dresses, sweaters, and accessories from many eras. Nice service.

MARBLEHEAD

O'ramas
148 Washington Street
Marblehead, MA 01945
617–631–0894
Hours: Wed.–Sat., 11–5; open Sun., 1–4, summers only
Owners: Cassandra Hughes and Suzanne Noble
Clothing from 1890 to the 1930s in a lovely romantic atmosphere. Lots of whites, some hats, jewelry, and shoes knowledgeably chosen by two special people.

PROVINCETOWN

Uptown "Strutters"
212 Commercial Street
Provincetown, MA 02657
617–487–0502
Hours: In summer, Mon.–Sun., 11–11; in winter, Thurs.–Sun., 12–5
Owner: Robert Garnett
Large store with nice selection of men's and women's vintage clothing from whites to Hawaiian shirts. Used denim also. Much in as-is condition.

ROCKPORT

Molly's Store
Bearskin Neck
Rockport, MA 01966
617–546–9041
Hours: Mon.–Sat., 11–5; open Sun., 1–5, June–Sept. only
Owner: Molly Turner
A small selection in a small shop of vintage clothing for men and women. Some whites and twenties dresses on occasion.

SPRINGFIELD

Hollywood and Vine
628 Carew Street
Springfield, MA 01104
No phone
Hours: Mon.–Sat., 1–6
Owners: Bruce and Muriel Mihalski
Deco furniture and home accessories combined with men's and women's clothing from the 1950s and 1960s.

Michigan

BIRMINGHAM

It's the Ritz
378 East Maple
Birmingham, MI 48011
313–646–3582
Hours: Mon.–Sat., 11–6; open till 9 on Thurs.
Owners: Frank and Debbie Caruso
A small, well-packed store with vintage clothing, toiletries, and some new wave.

DEARBORN

Cinderella's Attic
13351 Michigan Avenue
Dearborn, MI 48126
313–582–4672
Hours: Mon.–Sat., 11–7; Thurs. & Fri., 11–9
Owner: Heidi Lichtenstein
Vintage clothing from lingerie to coats, much of it from the 1950s. Some new wave fashions also.

DETROIT

Fabulous Second Hands
1437 Randolph
Detroit, MI 48226
313–963–3657
Hours: Tues.–Sat., 12:00–6:30
Owner: Marianne Penzer
A large shop with something for everyone from 1890 to 1955. Great accessories and hats.

ROYAL OAK

Patti Smith
511 South Washington Avenue
Royal Oak, MI 48067
313–399–0756
Hours: Mon.–Sat., 10–6; open till 8 on Thurs.
Owners: Patti and Jeffrey Smith
A selection of quality vintage clothing and jewelry from all decades, for men and women. Some new clothing too.

Missouri

ST. LOUIS

Alice's Vintage Clothing
26 Maryland Plaza

St. Louis, MO 63108
314–361–4006
Hours: Mon.–Sat., 10–6; open till 9 on Fri.
Owner: Alice Stauber
One of the first vintage-clothing shops in St. Louis with stock from 1890 to 1950, mostly for women. All clothing cleaned and repaired. Linens and laces too. Nice service from a helpful owner.

The Bear Shop
7533 Forsythe Street
St. Louis, MO 63105
314–727–0745
Hours: Mon.–Sat., 9–5; open till 9 on Thurs.
Owner: Margie Harper
Very nice, selective shop for women's vintage clothing from the 1890s to the 1950s. All items cleaned and restored.

Lucy Did It
54 Maryland Plaza
St. Louis, MO 63108
314–361–7516
Hours: Mon.–Sat., 12–6; open till 9 on Fri.
Owners: David Richardson and Skip Allen
Men's and women's vintage clothing from the 1920s to the 1950s with a glamour evening look. Accessories and Art Deco furniture, too.

Nostalgia Boutique
4900 Laclede
St. Louis, MO 63108
314–454–1900
Hours: Mon.–Sat., 12:00–5:30
Owner: Dottie Pashos
Anything in vintage clothing for men and women from bowling shirts to beaded dresses; sold in as-is condition.

Remains
5207 Hampton Avenue
St. Louis, MO 63109
314–351–6510
Hours: Mon.–Sat., 10–6
Owner: Kelly Stewart
Mostly 1950s or new wave clothing for men only, mixed with new designer clothing, such as Brooks Brothers shirts.

Voisin's
12¾ South Euclid
St. Louis, MO 63108

314–361–3100
Hours: Mon.–Sat., 11–9
Owner: Pam Voisin
Anything from the 1890s to the 1960s, mostly for women, sold in as-is condition. Some men's and children's clothing; also quilts and laces.

Wear Else
8109 Big Bend
St. Louis, MO 63119
314–961–1457
Hours: Mon.–Sat., 12–5
Owner: Larry Pankewer
Clothing from 1920 to the 1960s for men and women; sold in as-is condition. Some furs and accessories.

SPRINGFIELD

Lacy's Vintage Clothing
308 West McDaniels
Springfield, MO 65802
417–862–5002
Hours: Mon.–Sat., 12–5
Owners: Gayle Stewart, Jaque Smith, and Charles Jeffries
Men's and women's vintage clothing and accessories from the 1940s to the 1960s in a nostalgically decorated shop.

Old Friends
1204 East Elm Street
Springfield, MO 65802
417–864–7417
Hours: Tues.–Sat., 11–5:30
Owner: Kathy Mondrus
A small selection of vintage clothing for women, from the 1930s to the 1950s. Some new clothing.

New Jersey

DELAWARE

Wright Antiques
Route 46
Delaware, NJ 07833
201–475–5513
Hours: Mon.–Fri., irregular hours; Sat. and Sun., 10–6
Owners: Carol and Ron Wright
Shop equally divided between vintage clothing for men and women and furniture, from all eras. Nice service.

ENGLEWOOD CLIFFS

Very Victorian
22 Sylvan Avenue
Englewood Cliffs, NJ 07632
201–944–5100
Hours: Tues.–Sat., 10–5
Owner: Hope Schwartz
Specializes in Victorian and Edwardian clothing for women; some beaded dresses and accessories from other eras. All nicely displayed in a Victorian home.

New Mexico

ALBUQUERQUE

Second Chance
3500 Central S.E.
Albuquerque, NM 87106
505–266–4266
Hours: Mon.–Sat., 11–6
Owner: Larry Koch
Mint-condition men's and women's clothing from Edwardian through the 1950s; forties wool suits, shirts, dressy women's clothing. Also antiques, jewelry, linens, and collectibles.

New York

ALBANY

Daybreak
11 Central Avenue
Albany, New York 12210
518–434–4312
Hours: Tues.–Sat., 12:00–5:30
Owner: David Ornstein
Large stock for men and women, often purchased from estate sales, in varied condition.

BALDWIN

Deja Vu
821 Merrick Road
Baldwin, NY 11510
516–623–8719
Hours: Tues.–Sat., 12–5
Owners: Ruth Michaels and Orie De Luna
Comfortable shop to browse for men's and women's clothing and accessories mostly from the 1950s and 1960s.

BUFFALO

Fripperie
425 Elmwood Avenue
Buffalo, NY 14222
716–883–4188
Hours: Mon.–Sat., 12–5
Owner: Marcia Berg Burke
Vintage clothing and home accessories neatly packed into a small space. Linens and laces made into Victorian dresses and blouses. Men's tuxedos and morning coats. Clothing dry-cleaned and mended.

Zoot Suit City
1119 Elmwood Avenue
Buffalo, NY 14222
716–885–5020
Hours: Mon.–Sat., 12:00–6:30
Owners: Michael Gross and Carol Mansel
Large stock of clothing and accessories (ties, hats, belts) from the 1920s to the 1960s for men and women. Casual wear from the 1950s. Some never-worn clothing and some made from old fabric.

CAZENOVIA

Amanda Bury
Atwell Mill
132 Albany Street
Cazenovia, NY 13035
315–655–9253
Hours: Tues.–Sat., 10–5
Owner: Amanda Bury
A shop with a small selection personally chosen. Repaired and cleaned clothing mostly for women, including lace thirties dresses, Victorian jackets, and some Edwardian white blouses.

COLD SPRING

Mary Fauteux
104 Main Street
Cold Spring, NY 10516
No phone
Hours: Wed.–Sun., 12–5
Owner: Mary Fauteux
Mostly women's vintage clothing plus linens, jewelry, and wicker in a small shop.

GREAT NECK

Flirt
33 North Station Plaza
Great Neck, NY 11022
516–466–6260

Hours: Mon.–Sat., 10:30–6:00
Owners: Mitra Kaveh and Minou Moshiri
Nicely decorated shop of women's vintage clothing, from Edwardian to the 1940s.

NEW YORK CITY

Brascomb and Schwab
148 Second Avenue
New York, NY 10003
212-777-5363
Hours: Mon.–Sat., 12-7
Owners: Robert Brascomb and Thomas Schwab
A tasteful selection of clothing from 1900 to the 1950s for men and women. Always changing, always fun. Knowledgeable service.

Cherchez
864 Lexington Avenue
New York, NY 10021
212-737-8215
Hours: Mon.–Sat., 11-6
Owner: Barbara Orbach
Lovely selection of Victorian and Edwardian whites, in a country atmosphere. A good source for brides. Accessories and linens; some new clothing.

Early Halloween
180 Ninth Avenue
New York, NY 10011
212-691-2933
Hours: Tues.–Sat., 1-7
Owners: Joyce and Arthur Ostrin
An eclectic and theatrical array of vintage clothing for men and women. A small but chock-full-of-fun place. Lots of great shoes and accessories.

F.D.R. Drive
109 Thompson Street
New York, NY 10012
212-966-4827
Hours: Tues.–Sat., 12-7; Sun., 1-6
Owners: Wayne Mahler and Rita Brookoff
American primitive dresses, beaded dresses, 1920s cottons, along with whites. Lovely hats and purses from 1900 to the 1930s. Home accessories such as linens and quilts.

Forty's Wink
1331A Third Avenue
New York, NY 10021
212-737-9372
Hours: Mon.–Sat., 11-7

Owners: Candy and Wes Hunter
A collection of 1930s to 1950s clothing for men and women. Hawaiian shirts, suit jackets, rayon dresses. Some new accessories.

Good Old Days
351 Bleecker Street
New York, NY 10014
212-242-0554
Hours: Daily, 11:30-8:00
Owner: Maggie Ryan
Selection of men's and women's clothing mostly from the fifties and sixties, in a small shop.

Harriet Love
412 West Broadway
New York, NY 10012
212-966-2280
Hours: Tues.–Sat., 12-7; Sun., 1:30-5:30
Owner: Harriet Love
An eclectic and elegant mixture of vintage clothing for men and women in a modern and pristine atmosphere. A special selection of dressy clothing, beaded dresses, whites, Hawaiian shirts, and everyday wear. Lots of wonderful one-of-a-kind accessories. Exceptionally knowledgeable service.

Joia
1151 Second Avenue
New York, NY 10021
212-754-9017
Hours: Mon.–Sat., 10:00-6:30
Owner: Carol Caver
A nicely displayed shop with a Deco feeling. A selection of Hawaiian shirts for men. Women's clothing mostly from the 1930s to the 1950s.

One Woman
336 Columbus Avenue
New York, NY 10023
212-724-2223
Hours: Daily, 12-9
Owner: Joy Dicker
Vintage clothing for men and women. Hawaiian shirts, pants, jackets; blouses, beaded sweaters, and dresses. Some accessories.

Panache
525 Hudson Street
New York, NY 10014
212-242-5115
Hours: Tues.–Sun., 1-7
Owners: Barbara Collier and Ann Saposnick

A nice selection for men and women; Hawaiian shirts, blouses, jackets, dresses, sweaters, lingerie, and accessories.

Richard Utilla
112 Christopher Street
New York, NY 10014
212-929-7059
Hours: Mon. and Tues., 11–7; Wed.–Sat., 11–11; Sun., 1–9
Owner: Richard Utilla
A large store with never-worn but vintage clothing for men and women mostly from the 1940s, 1950s, and 1960s. Pants, shirts, jackets, coats, ties, and lots of shoes. Nice service.

Screaming Mimi
100 West 83rd Street
New York, NY 10024
212-362-3158
Hours: Mon.–Sat., 11–8
Owners: Laura Wills and Biff Chandler
An ever-changing selection of men's jackets, pants, and shirts, plus women's dresses, sweaters, suits, and (in winter) furs from the 1950s and 1960s mostly. Good displays. Nice service.

Second Coming
304 Columbus Avenue
New York, NY 10023
212-595-1447
Hours: Mon.–Sat., 12–7; Sun., 1–6
Owners: Elaine Levitt and Larry Rosen
A friendly store that sells furniture in front and vintage clothing for men and women in back. Bowling shirts, men's jackets and coats, some Edwardian whites in summer.

Shady Lady
2205 Broadway
New York, NY 10024
212-799-2523
Hours: Mon.–Sat., 11–8
Owner: Susan Kohn
A grab bag of vintage clothing for men and women; jackets, coats, printed dresses, and rayon blouses—some special, some in as-is condition.

Trouve
1200 Lexington Avenue, 2nd Floor
New York, NY 10028
212-744-4409

Hours: Mon.–Sat., 1–5
Owner: Linda Donahue
Women's clothing from 1900 to 1950. Specializing in dressier clothing, some whites, accessories, linens. Casual, homey atmosphere.

Victoria Falls
147 Spring Street
New York, NY 10012
212-225-5099
Hours: Tues.–Sat., 12–7; Sun., 1:30–5:30
Owner: Rena Gill
A collection of Edwardian dresses and lingerie combined with new designs in lingerie and clothing by Rena Gill. Lovely atmosphere.

NORTHPORT

Harbor Lights
110 Main Street
Northport Village, NY 11768
516-757-4572
Hours: Tues.–Sat., 12–5
Owner: Millie Allen
A nice shop with a personal touch on the North Shore of Long Island. Mostly women's clothing from the 1940s and 1950s. Some linens and accessories.

POUGHKEEPSIE

Madame Bovary
6 Garden Street
Poughkeepsie, NY 12601
914-471-1015
Hours: Mon.–Sat., 11–5
Owners: Karen Fishgold and Billy Frank
A small but cared-for and cleaned selection of tasteful and wearable vintage clothing for men and women. Dresses, gabardine shirts, pants, jackets, and accessories. Helpful owners.

North Carolina

CHAPEL HILL

Back Again Vintage Clothing
405 West Franklin Street
Chapel Hill, NC 27514
919-929-6221
Hours: Mon.–Sat., 11:00–5:30

Owners: Mandy Benz and Paula Press
A mixture of eras from 1900 to 1950 for men and women. Owners do musical fashion shows using their vintage clothing.

Ohio

CINCINNATI

Downtown
119 Calhoun
Cincinnati, OH 45219
513–861–9336
Hours: Mon., Thurs., Fri., 12–10; Tues., Wed., Sat., 12–6
Owner: Ossie Johnson
Clothing for men and women from the 1920s to the 1950s in a small shop.

Wearable Heirlooms
3161 Linwood Avenue
Cincinnati, OH 45208
513–871–3544
Hours: Tues., Wed., 1–5; Thurs., Fri., 11–5; Sat., 12–5
Owner: Sandy Clo
A small, elegant boutique with Edwardian and Victorian whites. Very selective and romantic. Some accessories. By appointment anytime.

COLUMBUS

Unicorn
2 Chittenden Avenue
Columbus, OH 43201
614–297–0129
Hours: Tues.–Sat., 11–6
Owner: Christiane Durtschi
Women's vintage clothing from 1850 to 1950; store directly across from Ohio State University. A nice collection of hats.

DAYTON

Feathers
415 East Fifth Street
Dayton, OH 45402
513–228–2940
Hours: Wed.–Sun., 12–6
Owner: Jan Tichy
Men's and women's vintage clothing from the 1940s and 1950s. Some forties furnishings and new clothing.

Oregon

ASHLAND

Birds of a Feather
52 East Main Street
Ashland, OR 97520
503–488–0176
Hours: Mon.–Sat., 10–5; Sun., 12–5
Owners: Barbara Brandt, Cherise Stull, and Debbie Cordova
Large store for vintage clothing, for men and women. Victorian and lots of forties clothing—suits, jackets, and blouses. Also accessories and jewelry.

EUGENE

Puttin' on the Ritz
1639 East 19th Street
Eugene, OR 97403
503 343 8938
Hours: Mon.–Sat., 11:00–5:30
Owner: Colleen Lillard
Lovely shop with men's and women's vintage clothing and accessories especially from the 1920s to the 1940s. Choice items and good service, in an old house.

PORTLAND

Johnnie B. Goode's Rock and Roll Fashion
832 S.W. Park Avenue
Portland, OR 97205
503–227–7772
Hours: Mon.–Sat., 11–6
Owners: John and Jeniffer
Vintage clothing for men and women from the fifties and sixties only.

Keep 'Em Flying
510 N.W. 21st Street
Portland, OR 97209
503–221–0601
Hours: Mon.–Sat., 11–6
Owner: Sandy Lang
Nice selection of vintage clothing from the 1940s and 1950s for men and women. Good basic day wear and some evening wear.

One More Time
1114 N.W. 21st Street
Portland, OR 97209
503–223–4167

Hours: Daily, 11:00–5:30
Owner: Name unavailable
An eclectic mix from 1900 to the 1950s for men and women, with some accessories.

The Shady Lady
823 N.W. 23rd Street
Portland, OR 97201
503–248–0518
Hours: Mon.–Sat., 11:00–6:30
Owner: Name unavailable
Vintage clothing from the 1940s to the 1950s for men and women.

SALEM

. . . And Old Lace
320 Court Street
Salem, OR 97301
503–585–6010
Hours: Mon.–Sat., 10:30–5:30
Owner: Elizabeth Southwell
A romantic shop with women's vintage clothing, mostly from the turn of the century, cleaned and pressed. Some buttons, lots of old lace and embroidery.

Pennsylvania

NEW HOPE

Katy Kane
8 West Ferry Street
New Hope, PA 18938
215–862–5873
Hours: Mon.–Sat., 11–5; Sun., 12–5
Owner: Katy Kane
A romantic shop for Victorian and Edwardian women's clothes; quilted petticoats, white dresses, blouses. Also quilts and pillows.

Trousseaux
Route 202 and Aquetong Road
New Hope, PA 18938
215–862–9177
Hours: Daily, 11–5
Owners: Doris and Edwin Netherton
A lovely shop with women's clothing, Edwardian through the 1940s. Decorative items, quilts, and textiles. Pleasant service.

PHILADELPHIA

A Touch of Panache
610 South Fourth Street
Philadelphia, PA 19147
215–924–1757
Hours: Mon.–Thurs., 12–6; Fri. and Sat., 12–7; Sun., 1–5
Owner: Linda Aiscowitz
Women's vintage clothing from many eras, including suits, sweaters, blouses, furs, and some whites from the turn of the century.

PITTSBURGH

Club Anonymous
284 Morewood Street
Pittsburgh, PA 15213
412–681–9387
Hours: Tues.–Fri., 11–6; Sat., 12–7
Owner: Paula Mahoney
Men's and women's clothes from Victorian to the 1950s in a boutique atmosphere. Well stocked with dresses, beaded sweaters, shoes, hats, and costume jewelry.

Rhode Island

NEWPORT

Romance of Arielle
4 Deblois Street
Newport, RI 02840
401–847–6615
Hours: Mon.–Sat., 12–5
Owner: Derri Owen
A small vintage-clothing shop for women only. Clothing from 1910 to the 1950s, in varied condition.

PROVIDENCE

The Cat's Pajamas
241 Wickenden
Providence, RI 02629
401–751–8440
Hours: Mon.–Sat., 12–6
Owner: Cheri Light
Vintage clothing spanning decades from 1910 to the 1950s. Some home furnishings such as Fiesta ware.

Texas

DALLAS

Eclectricity
2002 Greenville
Dallas, TX 75206
214–826–2195
Hours: Mon.–Sat., 10–7
Owners: Micheline Kerfonta, Blair Bryant, and Michael Longcrier
A mixture of vintage clothing for men and women from 1890 to 1950 in a rather large store. Accessories too. Everything cleaned and repaired except for sale items.

Faded Rose
2720 North Henderson
Dallas, TX 75206
214–826–7456
Hours: Mon.–Sat., 11–6
Owner: Joyce Baker
Vintage clothing for men and women from the 1930s to the 1950s. Hawaiian shirts, bowling shirts, lingerie, and dresses. Mostly day wear.

Lula's
3408 Oaklawn
Dallas, TX 75219
214–521–2852
Hours: Mon.–Sat., 12–5
Owner: Meredith Motley
Men's and women's clothing and accessories from the forties and fifties. Some new Indonesian imports.

SAN ANTONIO

String of Pearls
105 West Locust Street
San Antonio, TX 78212
512–733–1433
Hours: Mon.–Sat., 12–7
Owner: Debbie Reed
Men's and women's vintage clothing from the 1920s to the 1940s, cleaned and repaired.

Vermont

WAITSFIELD

Past Times
Bridge Street
Waitsfield, VT 05602
802–496–3086
Hours: Mon., Tues., Thurs.–Sat., 10:30–5:00
Owner: Cheryl McDonough
A small collection of dresses, blouses, and jackets from the 1940s; men's pants, suits, and shirts; some Edwardian and twenties/thirties clothing. Most in good condition.

Virginia

ALEXANDRIA

Great Gatsby
218 North Lee Street, Old Town
Alexandria, VA 22314
703–683–0094
Hours: Mon., 12–5; Tues.–Sat., 10–5
Owner: Joan Bradley Cohen
Edwardian whites, petticoats, dresses; some beaded 1920s clothing in a lovely atmosphere. Everything cleaned and restored.

Washington

SEATTLE

Delux Junk
3518 Fremont Place
Seattle, WA 98103
206–634–2733
Hours: Tues.–Sun., 12–6
Owner: David Marzullo
Large, very nice store carrying vintage clothing (some never worn), lots of interesting collectibles, accessories, and gifts for men and women. Lots of fun. Nice service.

Fritzi Ritz
85 Pike Street
Seattle, WA 98101
206–682–3163
Hours: Mon.–Sat., 11:00–5:30
Owners: Sylvan Johnson and Karen Selden
Good selection of clothing from 1900 to the 1960s for men and women. A mixed bag. Accessories such as hats, scarves, and jewelry.

Out of the Past
219 East Broadway
Seattle, WA 98102

206–329–2691
Hours: Mon.–Sat., 12–6
Owner: Name unavailable
Vintage clothing from the 1940s to the 1960s for men and women, in a small shop.

Sky King Haberdashers
85 Pike Place Market
Seattle, WA 98101
206–624–6137
Hours: Mon.–Sat., 11–6
Owner: Dan Eskinazi
Nice selection of men's and women's vintage clothing from the 1940s, 1950s, and 1960s, plus modern accessories, in a small shop.

Wisconsin

GREENBAY

Second Hand Rose
1505 Main Street
Greenbay, WI 54302
414–435–5729
Hours: Tues.–Thurs., 11–5; Mon. and Fri., 11–6; Sat., 10–4
Owner: Diane Starr
A consignment vintage-clothing shop, mostly for women, with items from 1920 through 1981. Large selection of furs.

MADISON

Bonton
302 State Street
Madison, WI 53703
608–256–3210
Hours: Daily, 11:00–5:30
Owner: Gerri Anger
Men's and women's vintage clothing from the 1940s and 1950s in a small shop near the University of Wisconsin. Newly designed hats also.

Passing Parade
409 North Francis Street
Madison, WI 53703
608–251–5508
Hours: Tues.–Sat., 10:30–5:30; Mon., 10:30–8:00
Owner: Bruce Edwards
Men's and women's vintage clothing from the 1940s and 1950s, including kimonos, lingerie, and daytime wear in four rooms. New dance wear.

MILWAUKEE

Sweet Doomed Angel
2217 West Farwell Avenue
Milwaukee, WI 53202
414–277–0829
Hours: Mon., 12–6; Tues.–Fri., 12–9; Sat., 11–6
Owners: Kathy and Jerry Fortier
A mix of many eras for men and women in a large store. Some in as-is condition. Newly manufactured clothing also.

Glossary

Aniline dye: A distillation of indigo discovered in 1826 that became the source of hundreds of modern dyes. Today aniline dyes are derived from benzine, a coal by-product. Aniline dyes made it possible to have brilliant, fast colors not obtainable from natural dyes.

Appliqué: A design made by sewing cut pieces of fabric onto the background material, sometimes with decorative stitches.

Art Deco: A design style or decorative art of the 1920s, characterized by bold outlines and geometric and streamlined forms. Epitomized by Radio City Music Hall and the sun-ray motif, Art Deco incorporated themes from cubism, Mexican art, ancient Egyptian art, and the machine age.

Art Nouveau: A style of fine and applied art, which appeared in the late nineteenth and early twentieth centuries, characterized by sweeping, curving motifs based on forms from nature.

Bakelite: The trademarked name of an early pressed plastic widely used in radio cabinets, telephones, and molded plastic ware, including jewelry.

Ballet length: Midcalf length, derived from the length of the older classic tutu.

Balmacaan: A man's knee-length, full-skirted overcoat with raglan sleeves.

Bandeau: Originally a narrow ribbon or jeweled band encircling the hair at the brow. In the early twentieth century, it referred to a narrow band sewn inside a woman's hat to make it possible to adjust it to the desired angle. Later in the twentieth century, it came to mean the first brassieres, which had a rather flat, bandlike construction.

Batiste: A light, very finely woven linen or cotton fabric; the French term for cambric. Used for lingerie, linings, summer dresses and blouses, and baby clothes.

Beaver cloth: A fur imitation, originally made in England. Used in coats, uniforms, and hats, especially top hats.

Bed jacket: A short, pretty jacket of any fabric—often silk, rayon, or velvet—to wear over a nightdress for warmth and elegance while sitting up in bed.

Bias cut: Fabric cut on the diagonal to take advantage of its stretchability for a close-fitting or clinging effect. Bias-cut dresses and nightgowns were particularly prevalent in the 1930s.

Boa: A long scarf or neckpiece, usually of feathers—preferably ostrich or marabou—or fur, tulle, or lace, that is worn wrapped around the neck with the ends hanging to the knees. The name is said to derive from the boa constrictor snake.

Boater: A man's stiff straw hat with a flat top and narrow brim, made of natural-colored straw coated with shellac. This traditional summer hat was most popular in the twenties. Picture Princeton boys, Boston bankers, and Mr. McGoo.

Bodice: Originally a separate top garment, it finally became attached to the skirt and went through many permutations of loose, fitted, tight-laced, and so on, through the ages. Now used to refer to the top part of a dress or, in vintage clothing, to describe the tight-fitted jackets of the Victorian era.

Bolero: A short, waist-length jacket, usually with no front closing and often with curved edges. Originally worn over a fine white shirt by men in Spain.

Bomber jacket: Hip-length men's jacket made of leather with a fleece lining and collar. Developed for wear in early, open aircraft (picture it with a leather helmet, goggles, and a long, white, fringed silk scarf, often called an aviator scarf). Also known as a "flight jacket."

Bouclé: A soft, knitted or woven fabric with a rough, nubby surface used primarily for women's sweaters and sports suits.

Buckram: Coarse linen or other cloth stiffened with gum or paste and used in linings to produce a set effect in a collar, sleeve, lapel, waistline, and so on.

Bustle: A wire frame or pad, resting on the rear and tied around the waist, to create a full, rounded elevation on the hips. Most popular in the mid-nineteenth century, when it was colloquially called a "dress-improver."

Camel's hair cloth: A combination of wool and camel's hair with a soft, brushed surface and a natural tan color; the fabric used in the traditional polo coat.

Cameo: Design cut in relief on a gemstone. So-called imitations are carved on shells or cut or molded in glass. They had great popularity in classical times, the Renaissance, and in the late eighteenth and nineteenth centuries. Queen Victoria was fond of cameo jewelry.

Camisole: An underbodice; formerly a corset cover. It resembles the upper part of a slip, snug over the bosom and looser at the waist, with thin shoulder straps.

Cap sleeve: A circular-cut sleeve, either very short or elbow length, with a wide, capelike flare.

Cashmere: The very soft, warm wool from the underfleece of the Himalayan Kashmir goat. It is either knitted or woven into cloth.

Celluloid: The first "plastic," invented in America just after the Civil War. Used extensively as a substitute for ivory in piano keys, knife handles, billiard balls, and so on, as well as jewelry.

Challis: A fine, soft fabric originally of silk and worsted, now made of wool or wool with rayon or cotton, which feels like a light wool. Used chiefly as a dress fabric.

Chemise: Originally a full, white undergarment of linen, cotton, or silk gathered onto a neckband with long sleeves ending in wrist ruffles. The chemise was visible at the neck, sleeves, or hem during many periods of costume. In the nineteenth century it was reduced to a simpler, sleeveless design. The word can now refer to a vintage undergarment or describe a simple, straight, waistless line in any garment—such as the "sack dress" of the early 1960s.

Cheongsam: A tightly fitted one-piece Chinese dress—often of plain, patterned, or brocade silk—fastened on the right side, with a stand-up collar and skirt slit up the sides to the knee or above. The cheongsam began as a long dress when it was invented in the 1920s as a compromise between Chinese and Western styles, but the hemline rose slowly and by 1947 was in line with Western fashion. This dress was banned in mainland China after the communist revolution in 1949, but it remains fashionable today in Hong Kong and Taiwan.

Chesterfield: Classic dress overcoat for men, characterized by a narrow velvet collar and fly front.

Chiffon: A dressy lightweight fabric of silk or a glossy synthetic; it is plain woven, slightly shiny, and softly draped, making it suitable for flowing, floating evening gown styles.

Chubby: A hip-length women's coat with full sleeves, made of fluffy fur or heavy fabric, that gives the wearer a slightly top-heavy look.

Circle skirt: A full skirt that makes a circle when laid flat. Circular-cut skirts were first made in the 1890s, when they were held in shape by haircloth interlinings from waist to hem. The circle skirt was revived in the 1940s and 1950s and was often decorated with appliqué work—typically a pair of poodles—and worn with a cinch belt.

Cloche: A bell-shaped, very close-fitting hat for women, popular in the 1920s.

Clutch: A small, flat, strapless handbag that can be "clutched" in the hand or under the arm.

Corset: A lace-up garment to shape women's torsos. Since 1500 B.C., when the Cretans suppressed waists with boiled leather corsets, men and women have tried to shape their bodies into the prevalent mode by lacing themselves into contraptions stiffened with wood, wire, steel, or whalebone stays. Victorian women wore fabric corsets with steel stays. The fashion for an 18-inch waist in the 1800s probably explains why many houses had small chambers near the front door called fainting rooms. The Empire and tunic styles introduced about 1912 freed women from armorlike corsets, and in the 1920s a boneless, one-piece, natural-form-fitting undergarment emerged. Modern two-way-stretch fabrics made it possible to shape without bones, although stays returned briefly in the 1950s with the "Merry Widow long strapless bra."

Crepe: A thick fabric woven with a crinkly, crimped finish. Wool, silk, cotton, and synthetics can be woven with a crepe finish.

Crewel work: Bold embroidery, also called Jacobean, worked in colored wools in varied stitches and filled-in designs.

Crochet: A form of chain stitching, invented in the nineteenth century, done with a single thread or strand of yarn. With a very fine thread, it is used to imitate famous antique laces; with wool or chenille, one can crochet sweaters, hats, shawls, and so on.

Cut steel: Faceted steel "gems" popular as diamond substitutes in the eighteenth century and often used in exquisitely made jewelry. By the end of the nineteenth century, cut-steel jewelry began to be cheaply manufactured as a substitute for marcasite. Cut-steel "gems" are bolted onto their backings—look for tiny pegs on the back of each one—whereas marcasites are set in prongs or glued on.

Damask: Cloth woven on a jacquard loom with a pattern that contrasts with the background by making one shiny and one dull and by using different weaves and sometimes different threads, such as rayon with cotton. All-cotton or all-linen damask is the traditional choice for tablecloths and napkins. Silk and wool damasks are used for draperies and upholstery fabrics.

Derby: A stiff, felt men's hat with a round crown and a small, slightly curled brim. Called a bowler in England, it—along with a tightly furled umbrella—is a traditional accessory for the British businessman.

Dirndl: A slightly full skirt that is gathered at the waist; derived from German or Swiss peasant costume.

Dolman: Originally the outer cloak of Oriental Turkish costume, a long full robe with long full sleeves slit to the elbow. Since then other cloak and jacket styles have been called dolmans. Today the word describes a sleeve style that is not set-in, that is full under the arm and tapers to the wrist: a sort of modified batwing effect.

Dress clips: Usually triangular-shaped ornaments, made of real and "costume" jewels, with hinged backs to decorate the neckline or lapels.

Edwardian: Special styles, usually very elaborate, dating from the reign of Edward VII of England, 1901–1910.

Eisenhower jacket: A waist-length, military-style jacket with snug banded cuffs and waistline, made with olive-drab cloth and button-cuff sleeves. Called an Eisenhower jacket because it was popularized by Dwight D. Eisenhower during World War II. Also called battle or combat jacket.

Embroidery: The art of ornamenting textiles by means of various fancy stitches with a needle and threads of wool, silk, linen, cotton, or metal.

Empire waist or line: Very high-waisted gowns—waistline just under the bust—with straight skirts. The term dates from the Empire of Napoleon I.

Enamel: Baked-on, smooth color used in better jewelry, especially—in modern times—during the Art Deco period. Cheaper jewelry imitated enamelwork with shiny paints.

Eyelet: Embroidered designs—usually floral—with small, thread-bound cutouts.

Faggoting: A kind of crisscrossed, openwork decorative stitch.

Faille: A heavy silk fabric with lengthwise ribs.

Fair Isle: A traditional knitted design from the Highlands and islands of Scotland fashionable for hand-knitted sweaters in the whole of Britain between the two world wars. The pattern consists of horizontal bands of small, complex, colored geometric designs—either overall or set in a plain background.

Fedora: A soft, felt hat with the crown creased length-wise and a soft brim. The prevailing men's style, and the one most often appropriated for women's wear; as in *Annie Hall.*

Flapper: Slang for young women in the 1920s who broke free from traditional restraints in dress (via short skirts, bobbed hair), manners, and morals.

Foulard: A twill-weave cotton fabric with a silky feeling and a small, all-over print. A popular necktie fabric.

Gabardine: A close, smooth-finish weave in cotton, rayon, or wool, used in dresses, coats, suits, and men's shirts. The boxily cut, long-sleeved casual men's gabardine shirt of the 1940s and 1950s is a vintage-clothing basic.

Georgette: A fabric of finely twisted silk or synthetic threads that has a slightly wrinkly surface and a cottony feel.

Godet: A triangular piece of cloth inserted for extra width or flare.

Gold: Pure gold is designated 24 karat, but most gold jewelry is alloyed with other metals for greater strength. In England before 1854, "gold" meant 18 to 24 karats, and after that, 15-, 12-, and 9-karat weights were used, each having proportionately less gold and more alloy. In the early thirties in the United States, 14 karat became the minimum standard that could be stamped gold.

Gold-filled: Metal wrapped with sheets of gold. This process is also called rolled gold. A lot of gold-filled jewelry was made around 1900 and can be very fine. Gold-filled items are sometimes marked 1/20 10KT, or GF.

Gold-plated: A thin film of gold usually electroplated onto the surface of another metal. Plated items contain considerably less gold than do gold-filled ones. Gold-plated or "washed" items are also referred to as gilt.

Hacking jacket: A riding jacket having a tight waist and flared skirt, with slits or vents at the sides or back and slanted pockets with flaps.

Handkerchief hem: A hemline consisting of triangular points.

Hand-screened cloth: Fabric upon which the design has been silk-screened by hand.

Harris tweed: Rough woolen tweed in subtle colors originally dyed and woven by hand in the islands of Scotland. Now Harris tweeds are usually machine loomed.

Hawaiian shirt: Men's sport shirt, usually short sleeved, in rayon, silk, or cotton, printed with any number of different Hawaiian or Japanese motifs in bright colors. The term originally referred to the shirts made in Hawaii, but now covers Hawaiian-style shirts manufactured in the United States as well.

Homespun: Hand-loomed, plain-weave cotton, linen, or wool fabric with a rough surface and small bumps caused by uneven thread diameters.

Jabot: A fall of cotton, silk, or lace worn at the neck to conceal the closure of a man's shirt (seventeenth and eighteenth centuries) or to "finish" a lady's blouse (nineteenth and twentieth centuries).

Jacquard weave: A method of weaving patterns or figures into fabric. The term comes from the jacquard loom, invented by Joseph Marie Jacquard in 1801, that made it possible to weave fancy designs into cloth. Jacquard weaves include linen and cotton damask napery, silk and rayon dress and drapery brocades, wool tapestry weaves, and men's silk scarves and neckties with woven-in designs. Any fabrics with woven-in patterns or figures beyond the simplest geometrics are made on a jacquard loom.

Jet: A hard, black form of lignite that can be highly polished. Used in costume jewelry and for beaded decorations. Especially popular in the nineteenth century for mourning jewelry.

Jewel neck: A high, collarless round neckline on a dress or blouse, so named because it provides an uncluttered background for a necklace or pin.

Jodhpurs: Riding pants cut very full over the hips for comfort while seated on a horse and tapering at the knee to become tight-fitting from knee to ankle to accommodate boots.

Kimono: The fundamental Japanese garment for men and women, square-cut with rectangular sleeves either small (*kosode*) or wide and hanging (*furisode*) and a neckband that forms a standing collar in the back and a flat border on the front edges to the waist. Kimonos are made of straight pieces of silk or cotton about eighteen inches wide (the width of the traditional Japanese loom) that are sewn together loosely so they can be taken apart for washing or cleaning.

Knickers: Short for *knickerbockers,* loose-fitting britches gathered in just below the knee, used for sports (especially golf) in the twenties and thirties and worn by small boys before they acquired the privilege of long trousers. Said to have come from Cruikshank's illustrations of Dutchmen in Washington Irving's *History of New York.* Also a colloquial English name for feminine underpants.

Lamé: A silk or rayon cloth woven with flat metal threads that give an over-all metallic appearance or serve as the background for a brocade.

Lapin: The French word for rabbit. American furriers often refer to rabbit skins as lapin, using the American pronunciation "*lap*-in," which may cause confusion.

Lawn: A thin, plain-weave cotton fabric, less fine than batiste, most often used in lingerie and summer dresses.

Leg-o'-mutton sleeve: A sleeve that fits the forearm tightly and flares from the elbow into a balloon shape, which is gathered or pleated into a fitted armhole.

Linen: A fiber obtained from the flax plant, plainwoven into cloth of any number of weights from very fine to coarse and nubby. Used in men's suits, women's day wear, damask-weave napery, and plainwoven tea towels, which are preferred for drying glasses because linen does not shed lint.

Lisle: Cotton yarn used in fine knits for hosiery, underwear, and gloves until synthetics became prevalent. Lisle is strong and holds its shape well, but it is not as soft and pliable as some other cotton knits.

Mandarin coat or jacket: A straight, boxy style derived from the Chinese, usually of silk or brocade, featuring a small, close, stand-up collar and "frog"-type fastenings.

Marabou: A soft, white, fluffy feather trimming used on hats, bed jackets, boas, and so on. Similar to swansdown, it comes from the tail and underwing of the marabou stork of West Africa.

Marcasite: A silvery substance made of crystallized iron pyrites, popular for jewelry, buckles, buttons, and so on, in the eighteenth and nineteenth centuries. Marcasites are set, like small gemstones, in better jewelry—often sterling—and glued onto cheaper pieces. Exists also in a gold color, which is known as "fool's gold."

Melton cloth: A stout woolen cloth for men's wear with a closely clipped surface, feltlike in feeling. Used for riding jackets in the most famous "hunt" in England, at Melton Mowbray, Leicestershire.

Mesh bag: A small ladies' handbag of flexible links of metal in gold, silver, or plated metal. A popular evening bag in the early twentieth century, colored enamel-look bags manufactured by Whiting Davis are an Art Deco classic.

Mildew: A thin, whitish coating appearing on cloth, paper, leather, and other surfaces, which is caused by a minute fungus and encouraged by damp and darkness. Usually appears first on greasy areas, even fingerprints.

Miser's purse: A small crocheted or "netted" purse

with a metal ring that slides over the top and down to the contents, making it difficult to reach any possible money at the bottom.

Moiré: Silk or rayon fabric with a watered appearance made by pressing with heated engraved rollers.

Moth damage: Holes in garments, especially wool, caused by the larvae of the flying creature that lays its eggs in warm, dark places. To avoid moth damage, put clothes away freshly cleaned and shake and air as frequently as is practical. Mothballs and layers of newsprint are reasonably effective in boxed items. Kill moths as you see them, because they may not have laid their eggs yet.

Mother-of-pearl: The shiny iridescent lining of a seashell, usually an oyster. Can be stamped out for buttons or more delicately carved into ornaments.

Muslin: Cotton cloth in a plain weave that varies from thin, light materials (batiste, etc.) used for lingerie to heavy sheeting of which percale is the top grade.

"New Look": The style, introduced by Paris couturiers following World War II, featuring calf-length skirts and very generous use of fabric as supplies of cloth returned to the civilian market. The style had a natural, rounded shoulder, a full bust, tight waist, and billowing skirts.

Norfolk jacket: Jacket worn by men and women for active sports, such as golf or cycling, featuring a built-in self-belt, trim, and capacious pockets. Introduced in the 1880s by the Duke of Norfolk.

Obi: The wide sash worn over a Japanese kimono at the waist.

Oxidation: An unfavorable chemical reaction caused by oxygen, affecting the natural condition of some materials, such as when metal rusts or fur turns reddish.

Panama hat: Usually fedora-style hats made from finely hand-braided straw in Ecuador, Peru, and Colombia. They became known as "Panama" hats because they were popularized by men who wore them during the building of the Panama Canal.

Panniers: Originally frames of wire or whalebone used beneath the skirt to extend the fabric at the hips (a cousin of the bustle). Later the effect was achieved by gathering folds of material mounted on the outside of the garment.

Passementerie: Originally a trimming of gold or silver lace. Later composed of braid ornamented with jet or metal beads.

Paste: A hard, shiny composition of fused silica, white oxide of lead, glass, and so on, used to make artificial gemstones, usually "diamonds."

Peplum: Formerly an ornamental overskirt, now reduced to a three- to six-inch frill or flared band around the waist of a dress or jacket. Also used to describe a short flaring jacket skirt attached to a tight waist.

Picot: An ornamental edging to lace, braid, or ribbon, formed of tiny loops of twisted thread.

Pin tucks: Evenly spaced, stitched-down, parallel folds, one-eighth of an inch or less. In other words, small tucks, either spaced individually or in groups, often used on batiste lingerie and blouses.

Piqué: Cotton or silk fabric with patterns of ridging (wales), popular for men's formal ties, women's dresses, separate collars and cuffs.

Pongee: A thin silk or sometimes cotton fabric with a rough, nubby surface used for men's and women's summer wear.

Princess line: A style of dress or coat cut in long gores, bodice and skirt together with no waist seam, fitted to hug the bust, waist, and hips and then flare to the hem.

Raglan: An overcoat, jacket, or sweater without shoulder seams, the sleeve going right up to the neck. Said to have originated in garments made for Lord Raglan, British commander in the Crimean War (1853–1856), possibly to conceal the fact that he'd lost an arm.

Rayon: A textile manufactured from cellulose (vegetable fiber). Invented in Paris in 1884, it was known as artificial silk until 1924, when new methods of making the product were discovered. Then the term *rayon* was used to describe all synthetic fibers, including acetate, which is made of cellulose and acetic acid. In 1937 the FTC ruled that only fibers made from cellulose alone could be called rayon. Early rayons were very lustrous and used principally for lingerie. From the 1940s on, rayon has been used in many weaves such as crepes, silklike fabrics, broadcloth, gabardine, linen textures, sharkskin, and jersey.

Redingote: A double-breasted outercoat with long, plain skirts cut away in front for ease in horseback riding. Later adopted as a woman's fashion in France. The name is a corruption of "riding coat."

Reindeer sweater: A general term for pullover sweaters with knitted-in Scandinavian designs, originating in imported ski sweaters, the first of which had reindeer in the pattern.

Reticule: A small bag, usually made of some woven material, for carrying on the arm or in the hand, used by ladies as a pocket or workbag. Could be daintily embroidered for dress occasions.

Self-belt: A belt made of the same material as the garment.

Sequins: Shiny little disks or spangles used to ornament dresses or sweaters, sewn on by passing a thread through a small center hole.

Serge: A type of twisted wool used for men's suits.

Shantung: A silk or rayon fabric with a nubby texture used in men's and women's sportswear and summer suits.

Shetland wool: Thin, finely twisted wool from the undercoat of the Shetland sheep of Scotland.

Silver plate: A base metal covered with a thin silver coating, usually by electroplating. Silver plate is common for flatware, serving dishes, dressing-table accessories, and so on, but it is almost never seen in jewelry.

Smocking: A decorative stitching that holds together material gathered into small pleats to provide shaping and adornment to a garment. Traditionally used on peasant blouses and often on dresses for little girls.

Smoking jacket: A man's soft jacket, usually of a dressy fabric, worn as a replacement for a formal-dress coat when a gentleman retired from the drawing room to enjoy a pipe or cigar. Probably worn to keep the heavy tobacco odor from saturating the dress garment.

Spanish shawl: Usually, black silk crepe shawl with brilliantly colored embroidered birds and flowers and a deep handmade fringe, standard in Spain in the nineteenth and early twentieth centuries. In the 1920s some were imported from South America and China. Later they were widely imitated in cheaper fabrics and inferior workmanship.

Stays: Strips of flexible whalebone used to stiffen and shape garments, usually at the waistline. Also a synonym for corset.

Sterling silver: A metal alloy of 925/1000 silver with the remainder usually copper for strength. Distinguished from German, or nickel, silver, which is any of various alloys of nickel, zinc, and copper with a silver appearance. Silver was very popular for jewelry between 1870 and 1880, made a comeback around 1900 to become a favorite of Art Nouveau jewelers, and has remained in favor as a standard jewelry metal.

Taffeta: A crisp, dressy fabric with a dull sheen made from silk or rayon. Spills often permanently stained taffeta because liquid can cause the sizing (stiffening) in the fabric to run, affecting the dye.

Tatting: A kind of knotted lace, made from stout sewing thread, used for edging and trimming.

Teddy: A one-piece undergarment combining slip and panties, made of rayon, silk, or cotton. Worn mostly in the 1920s and now popular again. Also known as a "combination."

Top stitching: A decorative row of plain running stitches, either hand- or machine-done, possibly in a contrasting color.

Toque: A small hat without a projecting brim or having only a small turned-up brim. Originally a small pad worn on the head to raise up the hair, colloquially known as a "rat."

Tortoiseshell: The polished shell of the hawksbill turtle, originally used to make combs, ornaments, and dressing-table accessories. Since this sea turtle is now an endangered species, the attractive brown, beige, and black patterns are successfully incorporated into many objects made of plastic.

Tuxedo: A black coat of formal cut and material used for slightly less formal occasions than a tailcoat (usually at home). Also called a dinner jacket. Worn with a stiff-bosomed shirt and collar but with a black tie and waistcoat as opposed to the white tie and waistcoat used with the tailcoat. Tuxedo is an American term referring to Tuxedo Park, New York, where the style was first introduced from England.

Twill: The most durable of all weaves, used most frequently for cottons and wool. The construction of twills gives an appearance of small, diagonal wales; also called the serge or diagonal weave. A twill pattern can contain even or uneven wales or form diamond or herringbone patterns.

Ulster: Men's double-breasted overcoat, first worn in the early twentieth century. It is distinguished by a detachable cape.

Velvet: A pile weave, lighter than velour. The pile may be pressed one way (panne velvet) or stand erect. Made from silk, cotton, synthetics, or a combination, such as cotton backing with silk pile.

Voile: A thin, transparent, loosely woven fabric of cotton, silk, rayon, or wool. Cotton voile, stiffened with sizing, is a popular dressy summer fabric.

Wing collar: Stiff-starched collar with folded-back triangular tips at the opening. Worn with men's formal evening attire.

Yoke: The part of a blouse, shirt, or the bodice of a dress that contains the neckline and covers part of the shoulders. The yoke fits the body and supports the rest of the garment, which may be gathered or shaped into it.

Grateful acknowledgment is made to the following photographers and organizations: Gustavo Candelas, for all photographs in the book except those listed below; Fred Seidman, for photographs on pages 1, 67, 126, 171, and 179; Kathleen Seltzer, for the photograph straddling pages 52–53 and those on pages 94 (right), 118 (bottom), and 144; Greg Kitchen, for the photograph on the top of page 86; Billy Jo Joy, for the photograph on page 186; Frank Simon, for the photograph on the bottom of page 62; and Jone Morris, for the photograph on page 26. Photographs on pages 23, 24, 25, 31, 61 (bottom), 77 (bottom right), 130, 164, and 185 are by Harriet Love. Photographs on pages 8, 10, 11, 13, 14, 15, 16, 18, 19, 32, 42, 69, 124, and 152 are courtesy The Bettmann Archive, Inc.; photographs on pages 166 (bottom left and right), 167, 168 (top pin), 169, and 170 are courtesy Robert W. Skinner, Inc.; photographs on pages 34, 36, 37, 38, and 40 are courtesy Christies New York; photograph on page 17 is courtesy Christian Dior, S.A., Paris.

Grateful acknowledgment is made to the following modeling agencies and models: Photographs of Gina Davis on pages 58, 60–61 (top), 65 (top), 66, 73, 87, 101 (left), 136, and 141 (bottom) are courtesy Zoli Modeling Agency. Photographs on pages 6, 78, 90 (bottom), 112 (top right), and 139 (right) are of Suzanne Srlamba. Photographs of Julie Myers on pages 49, 52 (top), 70, and 172 are courtesy Elite Modeling Agency. Photographs of Dorissa Curry on pages 50 (top) and 51 are courtesy Elite Modeling Agency. Photograph of Rochelle Redfield on page 46 is courtesy Elite Modeling Agency.

Grateful acknowledgment is also made to the following for use of clothing, shoes, and jewelry shown in photographs: Clothing shown on pages 62 (top), 125, 154 (top left and bottom right), 161 (top), 162, and 166 (top) is courtesy Portmanteau; clothing shown on page 62 (bottom) is courtesy Dynabell's in Scottsboro, Arizona; clothing shown on page 90 (top) is courtesy Early Halloween in New York; clothing shown on page 130 is courtesy Trousseaux in New Hope, Pennsylvania; clothing shown on page 114 is courtesy Marilis Flusser; shoes shown on page 155 are courtesy Joan Vass; all jewelry except the top pin shown on page 168 is courtesy Eileen Chazanof. All other clothing is from the collection of Harriet Love.

The painting shown on the top of page 86 is photographed with permission of the artist, Robert Kitchen.

All drawings are by Durell Godfrey.